"*The Awesome* David French i selling. It clari manipulation or degrading the purchaser and the presenter. Read and re-read its contents until it becomes part of you and then buy a dozen copies and give them to your friends. Both you and your associates will be the better for it. I have no reservations in recommending it."

- Dr. Peter John Daniels
Founder, World Centre for
Entrepreneurial Studies Foundation
www.peterjdaniels.com

"After reading this book you will know more about 'why people buy' and how to easily and successfully sell to them than 99% of all professional salespeople."

- Eric Wong
Senior Vice President, Capital One Bank

"For more than four decades, I have been selling controversial scientific ideas to people all over the world. Paul's fine book surprisingly is as useful for selling ideas as it is for selling products."

- Stanton T. Friedman
Nuclear Physicist, Consultant, Lecturer
Author of *Science Was Wrong*

"I loved reading *The Awesome Power of No Objection Selling* because Paul tells it like it is and then instructs, step-by-step, how to sell big, sell well, and develop a returning and referring clientele."

- Elinor Stutz, Author of
Nice Girls DO Get the Sale: Relationship Building That Gets Results

"The No Objection Selling concepts have been practiced by women in everyday life for generations. Women intuitively understand that helping others get what they want is the most successful way to get what we want. Paul's book points out that it is this understanding that makes the sale easy."

- Vicki Donlan
Author of *HER TURN: Why It's Time For Women To Lead in America*

"A new and exciting approach to generating more sales. Paul French offers a 21st century system based on superior listening and analysis."

- Stephanie Palmer
Former MGM Studio Executive
Author of *Good in a Room: How to Sell Yourself (and Your Ideas) and Win Over Any Audience*

"Rather than requiring a salesperson to memorize and master a multitude of responses to sales objections, Paul's book simply and elegantly eliminates them entirely from the sales process."

- Matthew E. May
Author of *In Pursuit of Elegance*

"If my children decided on a career in sales, I'd tell them to read *The Awesome Power of No Objection Selling* and then ensure they understood personal financial planning to be good stewards of the wealth that would surely follow."

- Linda Galindo
Author of *The 85% Solution: How Personal Accountability Guarantees Success. No Nonsense. No Excuses.*

"*The Awesome Power of No Objection Selling* should be on the must read and use list for all women whose job or business ownership includes sales. It provides better alternatives to help anyone involved in sales work more productively."

- Janet W. Christy
Author of ***Capitalizing On Being Woman Owned***

"An excellent book that takes a no nonsense approach to selling. The strategies discussed will do more than remove objections from the sales equation; the professional relationship that exists between customer and salesperson will be significantly enhanced, improving closure rates and client retention."

- Terence Hockenhull
President, Charteris Consulting, Inc.
Senior Program Designer
American Management Association

"Paul's book is a spirited reminder that selling is ultimately about service. This is not merely an aphorism or an ideal–in the 21st century, more than ever before, putting others' needs first is the most practical approach to success."

- James Strock
Author of ***Serve to Lead - Your Transformational 21st Century Leadership System***

"The No Objection Selling concepts are highly unique, new, not available elsewhere, and totally effective."

- Anthony E. Whyte
President, American Institute of
Management Technology

4

THE AWESOME POWER OF NO OBJECTION SELLING

How To Take 'No' For An Answer And Make More
Sales Than You Ever Dreamed Possible

Paul David French

The Awesome Power of No Objection Selling

Copyright © 2012 by Paul David French
All Rights Reserved

No part of this book may be reproduced or transmitted in any form or by any means, graphic, electronic, or mechanical, including photocopying, recording, taping, or by any information storage retrieval system, without written permission of the author.

2nd Printing June 2016
Printed in the United States of America by Gorham Printing
Centralia, Washington

Library of Congress
Control Number 2012900484

ISBN 978-0-9850998-0-0

Also by Paul David French
Six Figure Selling

"Progress comes from doing things differently in unpredictable ways."

Stanton Friedman

Contents

> **Warning!** Do not prejudge the chapters by their titles and skip ahead. The sequence is vital to discovering the secret to acquiring the awesome power of No Objection Selling.

1	**Advantage** - What This Book Can Do For You	**11**
2	**Discovery** - How I Found The "Magic Bullet" The Experts Said Didn't Exist	**17**
3	**Perspective** - The Way We Look At Something Makes All The Difference	**23**
4	**Objection!** - Are Objections And Rebuttals Really Necessary?	**27**
5	**Motivation** - Why We Do What We Do	**47**
6	**Conditions** - Why They Must Never Be Treated As Objections	**55**
7	**Revealed!** - The Secret To No Objection Selling	**67**
8	**Essentials** - Should You Really Sell The Need?	**71**
9	**Causes** - The Real Reason People Buy	**79**
10	**Prioritizing** - How To Separate The Wheat From The Chaff	**91**
11	**Quitting** - You Don't Have To Close Every Time To Be Successful	**105**
12	**Problems** - Sell Them On The Problem And They Will Demand The Solution	**113**
13	**Prospecting** - The Difference Between Prospecting And Selling	**121**
14	**Process** - A System For Selling Without Dealing With Objections	**139**
15	**Versatility** - No Objection Selling Methods Vary But The Principles Do Not	**155**
	Epilogue - The Final Step	**165**
	About The Author	**167**

Chapter One

♦

Advantage

What This Book Can Do For You

> *"If you don't have a competitive advantage, don't compete."*
> **Jack Welch**

Within the pages of this book exists the single most powerful selling concept known: How to sell more of your products and services faster and easier without ever having to deal with sales objections. "No Objection Selling" empowers salespeople to take "no" for an answer and make more sales than they ever dreamed possible, and you will become one of them if you do two simple things: Read all of the chapters of this book, in order, and as you do, take the suggested actions.

You probably noticed that this book contains no preface, forward, introduction, dedications to people I care about, or other preliminaries. I purposely went straight to Chapter One for your benefit. What you are reading is more than simply a book about selling, it is a tool for selling my ideas to you, and in crafting this humble tome, if I fail to demonstrate my understanding of the first principle of selling–which is that you care about you, not me–then I would not be qualified to write such a book, much less be worthy of expecting you to read it.

The benefit that you will receive from reading this book and incorporating its concepts into your sales approach is a newfound ability to easily sell more without ever having to deal with sales objections. You will close deals more quickly, more easily, and your customers will like and trust you more as a result of your non-confrontational approach. You will receive more referrals, more repeat business, and experience higher customer retention. This is the proven result of selling without overcoming objections.

I personally benefited tremendously from No Objection Selling when I become the top producer of a multi-billion dollar sales organization–the largest in its industry– during my rookie year in spite of the fact that I was, at the time, an introverted, analytical computer programmer with virtually no sales knowledge, experience, skills, or contacts.

You will read my brief story in the next chapter, but realize that it was the No Objection Selling process, *not* my personal skills or abilities, that resulted in the record setting sales and retention numbers. I had acquired a tool that enhanced my performance and optimized my sales results, and by reading this book and taking the recommended actions, you will do the same.

You have probably heard and read that selling is emotional. It is all about emotions, they say. And while it is true that emotions play an important part in the buying process, I have found that it is really the proper use of *logic* that is the key to successful selling. Buying *is* emotional, but successful selling is logical. The alternative would be to state that successful selling is *illogical*, and clearly, this is not the case.

I used logic to understand the emotions involved in buying, and then applied that logic to develop a *process* that successfully appeals to a prospect's emotions. What I discovered is that the act of "overcoming" or "rebutting" sales objections does *not* appeal to a buyer's emotions, and by eliminating that behavior, average and even below average salespeople (as I was) can achieve above average sales results quickly and easily. Such a process, tried and proven time and again, will be presented for you here.

♦ What's Wrong with Overcoming ♦ Sales Objections?

If you pick up any book about selling today you will probably discover that much, if not most of the material within its pages, pertains to techniques for overcoming sales objections. Yet if you have ever been on the receiving end of a persistent sales person's numerous attempts to close you on buying something you did not want, you can easily grasp why this approach is less than ideal. I am amazed how readily a salesperson will justify being confrontational with a fellow human being whom they hardly know solely because a commission is involved.

Unfortunately for these salespeople and the sales organizations that spawn them, a new day has dawned. The 21st century brought with it more sophisticated and demanding buyers who literally have the knowledge of the world at their fingertips. Permanent change is underway not just in terms of the kinds of products and services available, but in the way these products and services are bought and sold. The markets are shifting, the public has spoken, and even legislators are responding. Holdouts who remain committed to the traditional approach of overcoming objections are beginning to feel the wrath of these powerful forces.

The good news is there *is* a better way! Perhaps you have suspected this all along. Many people, upon discovering the power of No Objecting Selling, excitedly tell me that they instinctively knew that confrontation and conflict are *not* the best ways to develop a sales relationship, much less a sales career. They just needed someone to validate their beliefs, and give them the faith to act on what their feelings had been telling them all along.

So read this book, take the recommended actions, and soon you will be experiencing for yourself the awesome power of No Objection Selling!

Chapter Two

♦

Discovery

How I Found The "Magic Bullet" The Experts Said Didn't Exist

"If I agreed with you, we'd both be wrong."

You're about to read how I found what everyone said wasn't there. Then you'll learn how I used it to my advantage. Finally, you'll discover how to sell more of your products or services faster and easier without ever dealing with sales objections, for within the pages of this book exists the single most powerful selling concept known.

Please don't take that statement as some kind of ego trip on my part. I'm *not* taking credit for it. I didn't invent it, but I did discover it–for myself, at least–and not a moment too soon!

At the time of my personal revelation, I was an introverted, analytical computer geek attempting to sell auto insurance in Detroit, Michigan, and I was failing miserably. I was really down. I was so depressed and discouraged that I was on the verge of quitting selling altogether, and I would have quit were it not for a man named Jack Hempton.

You see, after seven months in the auto insurance business, I had just experienced my highest single monthly sales production of only six vehicles insured. Imagine only selling six car policies for the entire month in the automobile capital of the world!

The fact that I hadn't made any friends in my new job didn't help matters, and just as I was preparing to give up and quit selling forever, Jack Hempton, a fellow sales rep who happened to be working out of the same field office to which I had been assigned, reached out to me with a helping hand. Here is what happened:

Jack took me aside and told me to visit the Church of Today in Warren, Michigan, a suburb of Detroit. At that time in the 1980s, this particular church had the best bookstore in the state for purchasing motivational, success oriented, self-help materials. So I took Jack's advice and purchased three audio cassettes on selling.

While I was there, I happened to notice a flyer that announced an all-day seminar to be held the following Saturday featuring an Australian businessman named Peter J. Daniels. The flyer stated that Mr. Daniels would shake up my comfort zone, so I attended.

♦ From Failure to Success ♦

At that seminar, Mr. Daniels shared his proven system for identifying principles and developing formulas for overcoming any obstacle. This system had transformed him from a third generation welfare recipient and illiterate bricklayer into one of his nation's wealthiest businessmen.

Mr. Daniels gave me the confidence to believe in myself, or at least in his process for finding a better way, so I determined that I would stick it out in the sales business. That day, I made up my mind that somehow I would find a way to sell my products without dealing with sales objections, which happened to be my biggest obstacle to selling, as I suppose is true for most beginning salespeople.

And because I sought, I found! In less than 60 days, using the system Mr. Daniels described, I was able to identify key principles and develop a simple formula that allowed me to sell more of my products and services faster and easier than the hundreds of seasoned sales professionals in the largest auto insurance company in the State of Michigan in spite of my lack of sales experience, knowledge, skills, or contacts, and I was able to do it without ever dealing with a single sales objection. No Objection Selling also resulted in my achieving that company's highest client retention, which is the real test of long-term success in just about any business.

♦ The "Magic Bullet" ♦

Throughout my quest to find a better way of selling, I encountered many sales experts who tried to convince me that there was no "magic bullet" as they put it. These self-appointed gurus were always quick to point out that you cannot be successful in sales without skillfully overcoming sales objections. I discovered that the best response to that is simply, "Whether you believe you can, or whether you believe you can't, you're absolutely right." I think Henry Ford made that statement.

What these people failed to realize is that their egos limited their ability to have an open mind. They had many years invested in mastering the art of overcoming sales objections, and this skill was their bread and butter. For a novice like me to come along and suggest that successful selling might be accomplished without the need of their talents was threatening and insulting to them. They were proud of the manipulative abilities they had worked so hard to develop, and they had no interest in seeking an alternative. As one sales "expert" put it, "Removing objections from the equation would obviate the need for skilled, high-priced talent."

Yet I discovered that the exact opposite is true. It turns out that removing objections allows average and even below-average salespeople to easily get more business—and more repeat business—every time. This book will show you how.

I credit all of my success to the fact that I systematically applied the key elements of No Objection Selling to my sales approach without fail, and if you had known what an analytical, introverted, non-sales type of person I was when I began my quest, you would know that I speak the absolute truth when I say that if I could do it, you can do it too!

Chapter Three

♦

Perspective

The Way We Look At Something Makes All The Difference

> **Dolphins are so smart that within a few weeks of captivity they can train people to stand on the edge of the pool and throw them fish.**

You are about to learn how to see what others can't. Could this give you an advantage in the marketplace?

In Chapter Two I told you how I quickly and easily became the top producer of a multi-billion dollar sales organization during my rookie year in spite of my lack of sales knowledge, skills, experience, or contacts. I mentioned this not to brag about myself, but because it helps you to understand that I did not become successful by virtue of how great a salesman I was, because I wasn't great. I wasn't even good. I became successful by discovering a secret that produced immediate, amazing results. And now, having read my brief story, you realize that you can benefit at least as much as I did if you are given the same advantage that I acquired early in my sales career.

♦ Hiding in Plain Sight ♦

Many years ago, Earl Nightingale released a recording entitled *The Strangest Secret in the World* which for many years held the title as the highest selling spoken record. In it, he spoke of a secret that remains hidden in plain sight, thus making it a "strange" secret.

After sharing his secret with millions of people around the world via books, audio recordings, speaking engagements, and radio and television broadcasts, Mr. Nightingale's message was then repackaged by an Australian filmmaker within the pages of the bestselling book, *The Secret*, which describes the exact same "secret" that Mr. Nightingale spent more than a third of a century publicizing. Clearly, this secret must indeed be strange to be so widely known and yet still referred to as a secret.

The secret to No Objection Selling should also be obvious, because the solution is hiding in plain sight. In fact, it is often sensed by people who instinctively feel that the traditional method of selling by overcoming objections is not the best approach, yet No Objection Selling remains undiscovered by the vast majority of salespeople and leaders of sales organizations due to the paradigm in which their minds are trapped.

♦ A Different Perspective is Needed ♦

You see, our perspective is based upon belief structures we have formed over our entire lives. The "facts" that we have learned about human nature concerning selling were ingrained in us almost from birth by television shows, movies, advertisements, books, formal education, and casual conversation gleaned from friends and family who probably had no real understanding of sales psychology or the mechanics of selling.

When we became involved in business, these ideas were then reinforced by sales books, audio and video recordings, and training seminars we may have exposed ourselves to in an attempt to learn from successful salespeople. All of this created a bias toward what I call the traditional selling model, and this model has some severe limitations and drawbacks.

But if you will allow me, I am going to change your perspective so that you can see what has been there all along but has been missed by most of us. In this way, you will quickly and easily pick up on the No Objection Selling concept and be able to readily apply it to all of the aspects of your sales approach, resulting in your ability to sell without ever again having to deal with sales objections. You are going to learn how to take no for an answer and make more sales than you ever dreamed possible.

The next several chapters will lay a foundation for changing your perspective so that you will experience the paradigm shift necessary to grasp the No Objection Selling concept. Please do not become impatient and skip ahead. Vital elements of the secret you are about to learn can be found in each and every chapter of this book, and I do not want you to miss a single one of them.

Chapter Four

♦

Objection!

Are Objections And Rebuttals Really Necessary?

> *"99% of salespeople give the rest a bad name."*

How do you sell without ever overcoming sales objections?

I get this question quite often from people who have heard of No Objection Selling but do not really know anything about it. Often, their tone suggests a doubtful, defensive posture, more of a challenge than a sincere desire to be enlightened.

The traditional selling model is built around the idea that objections are an integral part of the sales process. In fact, salespeople are told to welcome objections, that they are indicators of a prospect's interest in buying, or if nothing else, they provide ammunition for the salesperson to turn the argument against the prospect to close the sale.

Yet many people, myself included, have learned how to successfully sell without ever dealing with sales objections. I believe that people who cling to the traditional sales model are confused. Let's look at these things we call objections for just a moment.

An objection happens when the prospect objects to something the salesperson does or says, either rejecting the salesperson's attempt to close the sale, or rejecting their attempt to lead the prospect down the buying path.

And by definition, if the prospect is objecting to something the salesperson did or said, then the salesperson must have done or said something that the prospect found to be *objectionable*. Do you want to make a living by being objectionable to friends, relatives, and strangers?

Most salespeople believe that an objection is any point of resistance that they encounter when attempting to make a sale. This is clearly too broad a view, because sales resistance in and of itself is not objectionable behavior on the part of the salesperson, nor should it be cause for such behavior. But it can cause trouble if the salesperson allows this and other points of resistance to trigger the "rebuttal response" that prospects and customers find so objectionable.

♦ One Hundred Would-Be Romeos ♦

Perhaps this example will clarify my point: If we were to ask 100 married men how they got the girl of their dreams, I'll bet we would hear a lot of different stories, but it is unlikely that even one of these men would say that they took their future wife out on a first date, wined and dined her, then intentionally insulted and offended her so he could come back the next day with candy and flowers to try to make up with her.

Would you agree that being so objectionable as to intentionally insult or offend someone with the plan of trying to undo the damage on the next date is not a formula for success?

But if we practice the traditional sales approach, which is to plan on being objectionable and then rely on rebuttals to undo the damage, we are pretty much using the same ineffectual method as our failed Romeo example, aren't we?

Why should the prospect ever have to object to anything the salesperson does or says? You don't really want to be objectionable to your prospects, do you? Is this really the best way to sell?

♦ The "Expert" Opinion ♦

Nearly every sales course or book about selling devotes much of its content to teaching how to overcome sales objections. Many books and training programs are devoted entirely to this subject. They are at best expecting, and at worst encouraging the salesperson to be objectionable.

The authors might try to claim otherwise, stating that when possible a salesperson should attempt to handle objections before they come up, yet they still tell you to have your rebuttals in reserve, ready to bring them out the moment the prospect puts up any resistance, and keep hammering away until you wear the prospect down. Their targets then react by becoming that much more averse to letting a salesperson in the door the next time.

In other words, the traditional process has such a counterproductive effect that sales reps must become that much more adept at manipulative techniques to penetrate the defensive barriers *caused* by their objectionable behavior, thus making it increasingly more difficult for new sales people to survive long enough to become successful.

Any time the accepted practice for a profession is detrimental to that profession, it really ought to be time to look at more effective alternatives, don't you agree?

Having earlier defined objections, let's quickly define rebuttals also. A rebuttal is simply a counterproposal offered up to rebut a prospect's objection.

I will be the first to admit that a persistent salesperson that is skilled in the art of persuasion and has memorized a rebuttal for every occasion may make a lot of money for himself and his company. The questions you have to ask yourself are: Am I willing to go to battle with people on a daily basis? Can I afford to invest the months or even years necessary to master that caliber of manipulative skills? Will it enhance or hurt my company's reputation? Is this really the most efficient and effective way to sell?

An informal study was conducted by myself over the years, and the hypocrisy it revealed was staggering. When asking hundreds of salespeople what they believed my chances were of selling them something that they didn't want, the answer was unanimous: zero! I have never found one salesperson who would credit me with the ability to turn their no into a yes. In fact, they usually let me know that they would not tolerate such an attempt. This demonstrates their lack of confidence in the rebuttal method of selling, as well as their disdain for being on the receiving end of it themselves, yet these same people credit themselves with the ability to sell in this manner, and they feel totally justified in doing so!

♦ A Child Shall Lead Them? ♦

Consider a recent column written by the publisher of a well known magazine devoted to achieving personal and business success. In it, he extolled as excellent examples of successful selling the tactics children use to get what they want. Specifically, he mentioned how a child acts at the grocery store when he or she wants ice cream. Behaviors such as pushing through stall tactics, relentless persistence, overcoming objections, handling rejection, not taking no for an answer, and continuing to ask for the order until they finally get what they want, were all listed as vital components to successful selling.

I'm sure you have no trouble envisioning a child and a parent bantering in a grocery store, the child coming back with a creative rebuttal for every "no" the parent offers up. But is a battle between a child and a parent really a good example of professional selling, or does it simply reinforce the negative stereotypes of the typical sales person?

If you ask yourself the question, "Why would a parent give in to their child?" and then carefully think through the answer, I believe it becomes self evident that childish behavior is *not* a good example for a sales professional to emulate.

There are really only two reasons for the parent in the publisher's example to give in to their child. The first would be parental love resulting in the desire to please the child. But can you make a living off of selling to only those prospects who love you enough to buy from you just because they want to make you happy? Of course not!

This leaves the other reason for giving in, which is to simply shut the kid up so the parent can get on with his or her shopping. Perhaps your prospects might buy from you for this same reason: To make you shut up and go away. The problem with this is that once you are gone, the reason for buying no longer exists. "Buyer's remorse" sets in, and the prospect is likely to cancel the order. In fact, this problem is so prevalent within the sales profession that when sales are conducted over the phone, sales organizations often use a sale verifier–someone other than the closer–to confirm the sale immediately after the close for the purpose of keeping the sales rep honest and insuring that the sale will stick.

Children can be effective salespeople when it comes to selling *to their parents*, but a persistent, self-serving child hardly represents a proper example for pro- fessional salespeople. Nevertheless, most salespeople agree with the publisher's perspective and support the use of such tactics.

♦ In Their Own Words ♦

The following are just a few examples of the traditional selling model. These are actual statements made by sales managers, trainers, and authors:

- "Always be closing."
- "Don't take no for an answer."
- "The sale doesn't start until you get your first no."
- "Don't give up until you get at least ten no's."
- "Use sheer animal dominance: The salesman is stronger in character than his prospect."
- "Use the prospect's own objections in a form of 'dialectical entrapment' to get a purchase commitment."
- "Interrogate prospects at length about their needs and then adapt your presentations so the prospect cannot rationalize a refusal to purchase."
- "You must have a chronic hunger for money and a state of mind which regards each objection, resistance, or obstacle as a challenge."

- "I know how to shake the money tree and make all the dollars fall off."
- "You need to passionately believe that they should have your product and feel compelled to sell it to them, no matter how much they resist."
- "Only a person with an extra dose of strong ego and a psychological need to take control of every situation barrels into a client eight times after the client has said no."
- "I build in twelve attempts that the salesperson will make, and I educate the salesperson in advance that the client will say no at least eight times."
- "All prospects lie, all the time."
- "Objections are a requirement to a successful sales day. In fact, without them, you are likely not engaging your prospects and customers."
- "Champions have almost an affection for even the peskiest objection."
- "If the prospect resists my attempts to let me manipulate him, then he's just not 'my' guy."

- "Never hang up on a prospect. You either make the sale, or they hang up on you."
- "I am a hired assassin."
- "Never let the truth get in the way of making a sale."

From a buyer's perspective, I believe I find every one of these statements to be objectionable. How about you? Is this really the best way to sell? Must we really be objectionable to succeed in selling?

One group of sales experts recently offered a list of their most recommended books for salespeople. Among the so called classics that promote traditional manipulative techniques was a book about covert persuasion, a book about the cult leader Jim Jones, and even Sun Tzu's *The Art of War* along with the advice, "You have to begin by seeing your prospect as the enemy. 'Attack him where he is unprepared, appear where you are not expected.'"

One sales book that is highly recommended by another group of experts includes the following chapter titles: *Head Game Warfare, The Attack Plan, How the*

Closer Manipulates the Customers to Think as He Wants, The Weapon called Reverse Psychology, Tactic Notes on Psychological Manipulation, The Closer Strikes, Going In for the Kill.

This kind of behavior can burn bridges with prospects and customers, or as I like to put it, "Leave a trail of bodies in your wake." Is this really how you want to earn your living?

All I can say is, after I began using No Objection Selling, I did not have time to deal with objections; I was too busy making sales.

♦ A Better Way to Sell ♦

I discovered a way to easily out-produce the hundreds of sales professionals in my company, and thousands of others in competing companies throughout the state, and I did it without ever dealing with sales objections. Was I any less of a sales professional just because I wasn't handling objections anymore? After all, I wasn't being paid per rebuttal; I was being paid per sale.

Additional support for the No Objection Selling approach comes from an exhaustive psychological study of thousands of professional negotiators from around the world. Conducted by a very prestigious global research firm, this study revealed that master negotiators rarely if ever offer up a counterproposal right after the other side has put forth an idea or argument.

Average and poor negotiators, on the other hand, were much more likely to immediately rebut an idea put forth by the other side with a countering argument of their own. The researchers also discovered that presenting a counter proposal at this most inopportune time triggers a defensive reaction that causes the other party to latch onto and own their idea to an even greater extent. This also inspires them to become very creative in finding reasons why their idea or argument is valid, thus escalating a simple difference into an emotional battle.

Some salespeople attempt to preempt or "handle" all conceivable objections before they come up by bombarding the prospect with information about their product or service, the majority of which the prospect really does not care about. This "shotgun" approach to selling is also objectionable, as it clearly violates the "So What vs. Me

Too" imperative, where you must prevent the prospect from thinking, "So what," when you are engaging him or her. You instead want the prospect to think, "Me too," which requires you to stay focused on only those issues that the prospect cares about.

Practitioners of other professions do not have the luxury of being objectionable to their clients. If you find your doctor, lawyer, or accountant to be objectionable, you will look for another one, won't you? People in these professions, and many others, have to bend over backwards to *not* be objectionable, and most of them do it rather well. So why don't most sales professionals do likewise?

I believe the answer lies in the fact that minds are like water in that they always follow the path of least resistance. It is much easier to accept the traditional sales model that everyone else uses and teaches than it is to develop a totally new one, especially when the experts convince you that there is no magic bullet and you must do it their way or you will fail.

When you observe salespeople making high incomes from using the traditional sales model, it is easy to be fooled into thinking that this is the best way to sell. However, when you consider that the majority of new salespeople wash out because they lack the skill or the will to deal with confrontation and conflict to make a living, you begin to realize that the traditional model fails far more often than it succeeds. This is not even taking into account the horrible but well deserved reputation the sales profession has acquired as a result of the impact this model has had on the public.

♦ Unintended Consequences ♦

Things seem to have reached a tipping point, and there has been backlash. Some time ago, the federal government began to respond to the voice of the people and took matters into its own hands, implementing more stringent Federal Trade Commission regulations for selling products and services.

Shortly after that, they created a national *Do Not Call* registry.

Then came the non-rebuttal statutes, where certain states prohibit salespeople from even attempting to overcome sales objections. Some experts are even saying that it is just a matter of time until we see a *national* non-rebuttal law put into place.

No profession's reputation is spotless, but when it gets to the point where legislators start passing laws against your ability to do your job, it is time to seriously consider making some changes, because when the government starts targeting selling, then any company that sells anything can suddenly find itself in the crosshairs.

Imagine if the government enacted a "total disclosure" law that required you to show your prospects a video clip of a sales meeting secretly filmed without your company's knowledge? How might the results of your sales presentation be affected by your prospect's ability to witness how they are spoken of by the sales managers and sales reps of your organization? From the vast majority of sales meetings I have observed, I suspect that the results would be less than desirable.

The problem is not just the government, however. Buyers are demanding a non-confrontational buying experience, and they are finding it online, on cable TV, and even on their cell phones. In short, 21st century buyers are demanding non-confrontational buying experiences, and if your company is not the first in its industry to provide it to them, then it had better be the second or third, or you will suddenly find yourself wondering why your customers have turned their backs on you, your competition has left you in the dust, and possibly even the federal and state governments are ganging up on you.

Take auto insurance, for example. I left that business in the year 2001 to form my own marketing and consulting firm because I saw the rise of the internet as a huge threat to property and casualty agents whose companies only offered personal lines of insurance.

When I announced my retirement from that industry, many of my friends in the business thought I was crazy for thinking that a computer could ever replace a licensed insurance agent. Of course, in retrospect, we now know better. People commonly get insurance quotes and buy insurance policies online without ever speaking with a licensed agent. In fact, many of my former colleagues have confided in me that their biggest competitor is not one of the many other insurance companies, but rather their own employer's web site!

♦ There is a Solution ♦

To remain economically sound, sales organizations must maintain customer loyalty. So how do we as salespeople, or leaders of sales organizations, confront these demanding customer attitudes? The solution is to open your mind to the idea that the traditional sales model is not the best way to sell, and refuse to accept the premise that you must be objectionable to be successful in the sales profession. To remain a viable enterprise in the 21st century, *how* a company sells its products has become more important than the products and services they are selling.

In the earlier example of showing your prospects a video clip of your company's sales meeting, we noted that it would probably be detrimental to making the sale. If your company utilized No Objection Selling exclusively, however, such a video clip, shown prior to or during your sales presentation, could actually be one of your company's most effective selling tools.

Refuse to use rebuttals under any circumstances. Commit to this, and seek a better way. If you seek, you *will* find. In fact, you will find it as you read, beginning with the next chapter.

Step One: Reject, without exception, the traditional selling tactic of attempting to overcome sales objections with rebuttals.

Chapter Five

♦

Motivation

Why We Do What We Do

Most people are unaware that one reason David killed Goliath was to avoid having to pay taxes. See 1st Samuel 17:25.

Traffic was light as I slowly eased my vehicle into the lane. Seventy degrees and sunny, the radio announcer was saying, or something like that. I was heading home, and as I drove my vehicle through a downtown intersection, something ahead of me caught my attention. Someone was waiting on the corner to cross the street, and as I approached, I could see the look of recognition on his face. He knew me, but I didn't know him. At least, not at first, but as my vehicle moved closer, I suddenly recognized his face, although I couldn't quite place it. In the few brief moments that elapsed as my vehicle crossed his intended path, I heard three words trail off as I was moving away, and the three words that he shouted at me were, "Buy my computerrrrrrrr!"

"Ah ha!" I thought, "Now I remember." He was one of the several salespeople I had spoken with over the past few days while I was shopping for my first computer.

I still laugh whenever I remember that moment so many years ago. The thought of it will probably live with me forever.

♦ Lesson Learned ♦

Within this simple tale of my encounter lies a profound lesson, for I saw in that computer salesman an important reason why so many salespeople struggle in their work or wash out altogether.

In each of us is a drive that pushes us to go off to work every day and make our living to provide for ourselves and our families, and almost everyone who sells for a living does so for the purpose of earning money. While this is not in itself a bad thing, allowing it to drive our selling behavior can be. Even if we are not as obvious as that computer salesman, we still may be revealing our desire to make the sale in a subtle way that communicates negative vibes to our prospects, and this can possibly cost us sales.

"Sure," you may be thinking, "But what can I do about it?"

The truth is that the best way to deal with this is to completely rethink your reasons for selling. This, in turn, will change the signals that you subconsciously send to your prospects.

For example, I failed miserably in selling *until* I changed my goal from making sales to helping prospects. Now, this may sound trite, and if that was all there is to it, it would not have any real power behind it.

I did more, however, than just say I was out to help people. I calculated the dollar value of the savings and benefits that each of my customers were projected to experience as a result of buying from me, and I added this number to a monthly chart. The idea was to serve the public in a specific, tangible way that could be quantified. This chart allowed me to identify, in dollars, the value of the service that I had provided each month.

Using No Objection Selling, my new priority became serving my prospect's best interests. I told them right out of the gate that the only time I worried about my commission was on payday when I looked at my check. The rest of the time, my only concern was to do what was best for my prospects and clients.

I did not say this as a selling tactic; I said it because it was true. I had made getting my commission the *result* of my labor, and not the *reason* for it, and what a difference this made for me!

♦ Contributors to the Cause ♦

I owe the idea of making my goal serving, rather than selling, to a man by the name of Jack Hempton, who mentored me shortly after I began my sales career. This concept had a tremendous impact on my success, and the resulting shift in attitude that I experienced helped me discover the awesome power of No Objection Selling.

W. Clement Stone, who built an insurance empire during the great depression, made this same discovery. His revelation also came to him in Detroit, where he began selling accident insurance for his mother's insurance agency. He stumbled upon the idea of not trying to sell every prospect for the sake of making a sale. Instead, he would add value to the prospect's time spent with him regardless of whether or not they bought a policy. This new mindset immediately increased his average sales per day tremendously.

Perhaps you were already aware of this idea long before you picked up this book. If you were, congratulations! You are already one step closer to mastering the art of selling more of your products and services faster and easier without ever having to deal with sales objections.

I can almost hear you wondering, "Is *this* the No Objection Selling secret?"

Not exactly, but your motivation for selling plays a large part in your ability to grasp the overall No Objection Selling concept, and is an important step in the discovery process.

♦ Appreciate the Value ♦ of What You Do

Do you really understand the importance of what you are doing for others when you make a sale? Comparing the price of a product to the corresponding sales commission may clarify things.

The overall amount of money the prospect has to fork over for your product or service is always going to be more than your commission. This means that, as far as money is concerned, the prospect has much more at risk than the salesperson, because the prospect is giving up the larger amount if he or she buys, but the salesperson only stands to gain or lose the smaller amount if the prospect does or doesn't buy.

To put it another way, the prospect has to want what I'm selling more than I want to take the trouble to sell it.

I realize that you may disagree with that statement. Most salespeople disagree with it, but carefully think about it for a moment, because it is an attitude, and it does not mean what you probably think it means.

I am not saying that I will only attempt to sell to people who are knocking down my door to give me their money. I recognize that selling requires some effort.

♦ The Bottom Line ♦

If you compare the price of the product to the sales commission, you will see that in order for the sale to take place, based upon the amounts the prospect and the salesperson stand to gain or lose, it is the prospect who must want to close the sale more than the salesperson does.

Or to restate, the prospect has to want what I'm selling more than I want to take the trouble to sell it.

I again point out that this is an attitude–a choice–and changing your mindset to believe that it *is* true will automatically result in more sales because people are complex and emotional beings. Your attitude towards selling will influence your behavior as well as your prospect's perceptions.

Realize that you are not a supplicant; you are a sales professional selling something of value. Your prospects must want it before they will buy it, and want is a powerful motivator. Recognize this and appreciate the value of what you are doing for them when you help your prospects get what they want.

To a traditional salesperson, this might sound like "the takeaway," however, this is neither a tactic nor a closing technique. It is an attitude; a point of view that pervades your entire sales approach.

Earl Nightingale once mentioned that if you try to catch a butterfly, it will elude you, but if you ignore it, it will settle on your shoulder. This concept seems to perfectly apply to selling. If your prospect detects subtle vibes or even a hint of desperation, you can lose the leverage you have as a person who can serve them by giving them what they want.

They say that there is no force more powerful than a made-up mind. Determination will *determine* your results. Make up your mind that the prospect has to want what you're selling more than you want to take the trouble to sell it. This statement must be true *for you* for it to do you any good. Promise yourself, here and now, that you will adopt this mindset as it applies to selling your products and services.

Step Two: Decide that the prospect has to want what you're selling more than you want to take the trouble to sell it.

Chapter Six

♦

Conditions

Why They Must Never Be
Treated As Objections

> **When tempted to fight fire with fire, remember
> that the fire department usually uses water.**

My six children owe their existence to the principle covered in this chapter. You will soon discover why as you read.

At least part of the reason salespeople believe that they must handle objections with rebuttals is because they often confuse objections with conditions.

Earlier, we defined an objection as something the salesperson does or says that the prospect finds objectionable.

A condition, on the other hand, is something that has to be satisfied before the prospect will decide to buy. All buyers have conditions. They may be negotiable, or not, but conditions should be discussed and agreed upon before you ever ask for a commitment.

55

Traditional salespeople usually treat conditions as objections, attempting to overcome the condition with rebuttals to get the prospect to accept salesperson's position. I've even seen sales trainers list conditions as a type of sales objection.

The so-called "price objection" is quite possibly the most common of these, but it should not be, because rarely, if ever, do prospects object to the price of a product or service. Allow me to demonstrate:

Did you know that a Boeing 777F wide-body passenger jetliner costs 300 million dollars?

I have asked that question of countless people, mostly salespeople, and I have never had a single person object to that price.

But if I follow up with efforts to convince them that they need to buy one, suddenly, here come the objections!

Are they objecting to the price? Of course not. They're objecting to my behavior, because attempting to persuade someone to buy something they don't want or at a price they deem higher than the value of the product or service is highly objectionable.

The price should never be the cause for an objection, but the amount they can afford, or are willing to pay, is always a valid condition. It's how and when you address their conditions that determines whether or not you're being objectionable.

If the traditional salesperson waits until he asks for the order to discover the price issue, then he typically attempts to close with a series of rebuttals, each designed to try to build the value higher in the prospect's mind until it exceeds the price of the product.

This method can work at times, but it has several drawbacks. Although some sales people enjoy the challenge of getting someone to pay more than he or she initially intended, it requires extra time and effort to make the sale, and completely wastes all of the time if the sale is lost. Often there is buyer's remorse, where the sale is cancelled later. Even if the sale sticks, however, buyer's remorse can prevent the salesperson from getting referrals and repeat sales. This is why you must address their conditions before you attempt the close.

How much are you willing to spend? What color do you want? When do you want it delivered? These are not objections, but a salesperson will end up treating them as such if he tries to get a decision before he satisfies the prospect's conditions.

Rarely can a salesperson satisfy every condition the prospect initially brings into the buying process, but buyers understand this, and conditions need not result in points of resistance or objections, and they will not if the salesperson understands what conditions are and addresses them in a timely and professional manner.

♦ Avoid Unnecessary Sales Resistance ♦

Imagine a hitchhiker, somewhere in Texas, trying to thumb a ride on a two lane highway. He is walking south along the shoulder of the southbound lane. He is carrying a sign that says, "Mexico or Bust." That sign indicates the hitchhiker's condition. He wants to go south to Mexico. If you drove up in the northbound lane and told him to get in, he would probably put up some resistance, because you are currently heading north, and he wants to go south. If you tell him that you are turning

58

around, and he gets in, but you fail to head south, you would suddenly be bombarded with objections!

Why? Because he does not perceive that you respect his conditions or intend to satisfy them. Buyers will resist if they believe that you are trying to take them somewhere they do not wish to go, but they will not resist if they perceive that you are taking them where they do wish to go.

Perhaps you are just going north because your vehicle is low on fuel, and you remembered that the only gas station within reach is a couple of miles north. If you fail to inform your hitchhiker of this, however, you may be in for a lot worse than a little verbal abuse. On the other hand, if you enlighten him on your predicament, he will go along and may even offer to pitch in a few bucks for fuel.

♦ When Not to Ask for the Order ♦

If you have ever watched a courtroom drama on TV or in the movies, they always say that you should never ask a question of someone on the witness stand unless you already know what their answer will be.

This principle exists for a very good reason, as the following story illustrates:

In the late 1940's, a small town prosecutor called his first witness to the stand, a frail looking elderly woman. After she was sworn in, he began his line of questioning with a simple query:

"Ma'am, do you know who I am?"

"Of course I know you. You're Bobby Thompson. I've known you since you were a little boy in my second grade class. You were a good-for-nothing trouble maker, and not very bright. Still aren't. You were held back twice in school, and you barely passed the bar exam with one point to spare. You tell lies, you cheat on your wife, and you abuse people's trust while making them think you're a saint. Yes, I know who you are alright."

Shocked and stunned, the lawyer tried to divert attention away from himself by pointing to the defense attorney and asking, "Do you recognize that man sitting there?"

"You know I do," she shot back. "He and you were thick as thieves when you two were little, and he's even worse than you are. He's a lazy drunk who cheats on his taxes and has a gambling problem. He runs around on his wife and has had two children with other women, one of them being your wife."

Both men were red faced and speechless.

Suddenly, the judge ordered a sidebar. Speaking to both lawyers in a whisper, he warned them, "If either of you morons asks her if she knows me, I'll send you both to the gas chamber!"

Likewise, a salesperson should not ask for the order unless he or she already knows that the answer will be yes.

Attempting to close before the prospect is ready to buy is highly objectionable behavior. It is important to know that your prospect is ready to become a customer before you attempt to close the sale.

I define the close as the logical conclusion to an effective and timely sales presentation. It is the point where the prospect makes it clear to the salesperson that he or she is committed to making the purchase so that the details of the purchase can be settled. In order for the close to be logical and easy, the prospect must be mentally prepared to buy.

When I was ready to get married, I did not have to ask my future wife if she would marry me. I used the No Objection Selling approach on her, so she was ready to marry me before I ever asked her. I already knew that she wanted to marry me because we had discussed the details of our wedding on several occasions prior to my giving her the ring which made the engagement official.

The ladies reading this might think that my approach was not very romantic, and you may be right, but it was the romance prior to the actual engagement that made the engagement easy–and possible! In other words, applying this approach to selling products and services will allow you to sell without ever dealing with objections. No Objection Selling makes the close easy, as it simply becomes the logical conclusion to your sales presentation.

◆ Never Assume the Sale ◆

I once had a salesperson lead me through a long list of questions, each of which I answered truthfully, offering no resistance because the salesperson never required a decision from me. When the salesperson had completed her inquisition and informed me that she would be switching my phone service to a new carrier, I pointed out to her that she never asked me if I wanted to switch my service. She then asked me and I replied, "No." She had wasted all of her time with a non-buyer.

When the prospect has made it clear that he or she is ready to become a customer, you simply begin settling the details. If, however, you *believe* that they are ready, but they have not explicitly stated such, it is important that you confirm this before you begin to write up the order. Never assume the sale.

Traditional sales training usually places a high value on the assumptive close, but if you really believe that you can trick someone into buying simply by walking them through the purchase agreement, then you have only tricked yourself. That technique only works on prospects who are already sold anyway, but it can destroy a sale if used on a prospect who is not mentally prepared to buy. And it is a complete waste of time when used on a non-buyer.

Assuming the sale is never appropriate. We have all been told what happens when we "ass u me," haven't we?

Always confirm their desire to commit before you begin settling the details.

In Step One you rejected the traditional selling model in favor of never being objectionable again. We will discuss in detail exactly how to do this, but the important thing is that you committed to forgoing the rebuttal method of selling forever, which leaves you no choice but to discover a better way. As necessity is the mother of invention, the better way will reveal itself shortly.

In Step Two you determined that the prospect has to want what you're selling more than you want to take the trouble to sell it. If you have made up your mind on this point, you will subconsciously begin to alter your selling behavior in accordance with this new belief, which will in turn automatically improve your sales results for the better.

The next chapter is completely bogus. It was inserted into this book to catch anyone who may have read the table of contents and skipped ahead. Since you are reading this, you did not skip ahead. Congratulations! You are awarded the Blue Ribbon of Patience, the Gold Medal of Discipline, and the Iron Cross of Restraint. Proceed to Chapter Eight (or you may satisfy your curiosity and read Chapter Seven, just for kicks).

Step Three: Commit to never treating a condition as an objection. Always identify a prospect's conditions and negotiate a satisfactory settlement before you attempt to close the sale.

Chapter Seven

♦

Revealed!

The Secret to No Objection Selling

> **Following his speech, the President of the United States was shaking hands with a couple when the wife, who was a fan of the X-Files, asked the president if there really were alien bodies at Area 51. The President answered, "I'd tell you, but then I'd have to kill you."**
>
> **The wife replied, "Then tell my husband."**

Now that you have read chapters one through six, you are ready to learn the true secret of No Objection Selling.

Take the secret word that was revealed in Chapter One and remove the second and fourth consonants. Next, take the secret word from Chapter Two and write out every other letter, backwards, beginning with M. Leave out the W.

If you are totally confused, it is because this chapter is completely bogus. A note at the end of Chapter Six instructs you to skip to Chapter Eight. Sorry that you didn't get the memo.

Okay, don't be angry with me. It's just an inside joke for those who took my advice and read the chapters sequentially. Please don't take it personally. The warning at the top of the table of contents pretty much guaranteed that you'd read this chapter first anyway.

I really want you to benefit from the No Objection Selling approach, so if you're just thumbing through this book trying to decide whether or not to buy it, if the many terrific endorsements have not done the trick, go ahead and read Chapter One. It gets straight to the heart of the issue, pointing out why overcoming objections is really a bad idea, how doing so is costing you sales, and how you can learn to take no for an answer and make more sales than you ever dreamed possible.

Before you go back to Chapter One, however, see if you can identify with Laura in the story below:

A sales manager was complaining to his secretary about Laura, one of his sales reps. After sending Laura out to fetch some sandwiches for lunch, he griped, "Laura never follows instructions. I'm amazed that she's lasted as long as she has. I doubt that she'll even get our lunch order right."

Just then, the door flew open, and in bounced Laura. "You'll never guess what just happened!" she shouted. "I ran into Donald Trump down at the deli. We got to talking and he gave me an order for ten million dollars!"

"See," complained the sales manager, "What did I tell you? Laura forgot the sandwiches."

Chapter Eight

♦

Essentials

Should You Really Sell The Need?

> You do not NEED a parachute to skydive, however, most skydivers WANT a parachute so they can come back and do it again.

You're about to discover the most powerful force governing human behavior. Can you use it to help you sell your products and services?

There are many needs in life. Everyone has needs, and most everyone has the same or very similar needs.

If you were to look into the checkbooks and credit card statements of 100 people, you would find that they all share many things. Payments to the electric company, the phone company, grocery stores and gas stations would all be present. Auto and home insurance, water bill, rent or mortgage payments would also be there.

These needs are commonalities among the most diverse of people. I believe it is safe to say that our needs are what make us the same.

If this is true, if our needs make us the same, then what makes us different? Would it be fair to suggest that it is our *wants* that define our differences?

Think about it. If you were to examine those same 100 checkbooks and credit card statements, you would find common needs, but if you separated out the luxuries, or *wants*, I think you will agree that you would see very different expenditures for our 100 subjects.

This leads to the point of appealing to the want, or desire, rather than the need.

I have heard and read hundreds of times over the years that the secret to selling is to sell the need. It is amazing how many sales books and training courses push this idea. Sell the need, they say. Yet, that idea goes against the grain of well known and proven axioms such as, "Sell the sizzle, not the steak," and, "You can lead a horse to water, but you can't make him drink."

You can convince people that they *need* something, but that does not mean that they will buy it. If someone really *wants* something, however, he or she will find a way to get it, whether they need it or not.

♦ Forgoing Needs to Satisfy Wants ♦

I discovered early in my selling career that people will forgo their needs but they will move heaven and earth to get what they want.

I am going to restate that, because this is an important key to the No Objection Selling approach: People will forgo their needs but they will move heaven and earth to get what they want.

Having doubts about this concept? Consider that most people's largest investment and single biggest monthly payment is usually the mortgage. Do people really need to *own* a home, or could they rent?

The fact is, in most affluent societies, people spend far more money on things they do not need than on things they do need. People will forgo their needs but they will move heaven and earth to get what they want.

Would you agree that oxygen is a need? How about food and water? Yet every day, people permanently deprive themselves of these essential ingredients for living by ending their lives. Suicide is one of the highest causes of death among young people in several cultures around the world.

What does this mean?

It means that on a daily basis, otherwise healthy people choose to solve a temporary problem with a permanent solution by depriving themselves of their needs in favor of a misguided want.

I realize that this is an extreme example, but it demonstrates the extremes to which people will go to satisfy their wants over their needs.

Where selling and buying are concerned, I can give you a more common example. We all need to breathe clean air for good health. Yet millions of people light up cigarettes every day and pollute their lungs with nicotine, carbon monoxide and other toxins. Why? Because they want to. Some people might say that they need it, but we know better. They did not need it before they started smoking, and they will not need it after they quit, as so many decide to do.

The reality is, they want it, and they will go to extremes to get what they want, including standing outside in the cold or rain if the building does not have a smoking section, and depriving themselves of substantial amounts of money to pay for their habit. People will do and endure some amazing things to get what they want.

How about food? Our bodies need good nutrition to be healthy, yet many people deprive their bodies of what they need in favor of unhealthy, chemically laced junk food and snacks. You can usually spot these people a block away. If you happen to be one of them, I don't mean to offend, I am just pointing out the facts. People will forgo their needs but they will move heaven and earth to get what they want.

If this principle is true to the extent that people will go so far as to harm themselves or even die as a result of satisfying their wants, then this is truly a powerful principle, one that we as salespeople should understand and utilize. Go *with* the flow, and harmonize with this principle, do not try to fight it.

Rarely will your product or service be the only one on the market that can meet your prospect's needs, because needs are rather basic. This is another reason to concentrate on what your prospects want. People will move heaven and earth to get what they want, which means that they will help you sell them *if* they perceive that you are serving them in the capacity of helping them to get what they want. Always focus on their wants.

Right here and now, as you read this, make up your mind that you are never again going to "sell the need." Instead, find out what people want and appeal to that. Tell yourself, "I only care about what the prospect wants."

And how do you find out what they want? Ask them! They will not hesitate to tell you. I also learned long ago that people might clam up when you try to lead them down a selling path with questions designed to get them to say yes and direct them to the result *you* want, but they usually open right up when you ask them to talk about what *they* want.

♦ Sometimes Less is More ♦

This non-confrontational approach became part of the *total solution package* that I was selling, and it greatly enhanced the prospect's desire to buy from me, because buyers want a non-confrontational buying experience. They will even settle for a little less on the product side in terms of price, features, and benefits if they perceive that they are getting more from their buying experience and from future dealings with the salesperson or the salesperson's company.

It is worth stating again: People will forgo their needs but they will move heaven and earth to get what they want. Memorize this, and make it your mantra for helping people to buy from you.

In Step One you made up your mind to never use rebuttals as a selling tactic.

In Step Two you determined that the prospect must want what you are selling more than you want to take the trouble to sell it.

In Step Three you recognized the importance of conditions, and determined never to treat them as objections.

Now add to these the realization that people will forgo their needs but they will move heaven and earth to get what they want. Endeavor to get to the heart of what your prospects want, what they *really* want, and then show them how buying your product or service from you will give it to them.

> **Step Four: Determine never again to sell the need. Realize that people will forgo their needs but they will move heaven and earth to get what they want.**

Chapter Nine

◆

Causes

The Real Reason People Buy

> *"Shallow men believe in luck. Strong men believe in cause and effect."*
>
> **Ralph Waldo Emerson**

I have asked hundreds of salespeople the following question, and I would like to pose this question to you also. The question is, "Why do people buy?"

Since I am not there with you to get your opinion, I will list the four most common responses I have heard over the years:

Because they like me.
Because they trust me.
Because they need what I am selling.
Because I make them buy it.

About 98% of all the answers I have received to this question over the years fit one of these four responses. Was your answer one of them also?

Let's quickly address each of these most common beliefs that salespeople have for why people buy, starting with the idea that people buy because they like you.

I recently read something in a famous book on selling that I have often heard stated over the years: "People are more likely to buy from a friend than a salesman."

I'm not going to argue against this idea, because it may be true that people would rather buy from a friend, provided that friend is selling something the prospect *wants*. If the friend is not selling something that is wanted, however, rarely will the friendship produce a lasting customer. This is evidenced by the documented 98% failure rate of home-based multilevel or network marketing businesses that involve primarily selling products to friends and relatives.

The proof of this is in your answer to this question: Does everybody who likes you buy from you?

As for myself, many people like me, but they do not all buy from me, because they do not all want what I am selling. This is true, I believe, for pretty much everyone. Based on this fact, we can eliminate the idea of people liking you as the reason—or cause–for someone buying your product or service. It may actually happen from time to time, but in general, people do not buy from someone solely because they like the salesperson.

How about the second reason on our list, that being trust? Does everybody who trusts you buy from you? Is trusting someone, in and of itself, reason enough to buy what they are selling?

I buy things from people whom I neither like nor trust all the time, because I do not know anything about them. The fact is, most of my purchases take place where the people who help me buy or who ring up my order are complete strangers to me, and I'll bet that is the case with you as well.

Take banks, for example. Banking is a business where trust would seem to be paramount. I trust my banks with my money, but I don't really trust them or the people who work there any more or less than I trust their competitors. I chose those banks primarily for their lower fees or convenient online banking features. After all, I don't know those people very well, so how can I really trust them?

It is true that if the prospect has reason to feel that a company or salesperson is *untrustworthy*, then this can become a "landmine" that gets in the way of a sale, but trust in and of itself is not a reason for buying the vast majority of products and services that we buy, is it?

Then there's the third reason on our list, but we covered the misnomer of buying based on need in the last chapter. But on the outside chance that you need a little more information on this point, consider the following true story:

While observing a sales presentation for cutlery, I witnessed a sales rep give an in-home presentation to a lady who had recently received a new set of cutlery as a gift. It was a different brand, and a good one, yet at the conclusion of the presen-tation, without any hesitation, she placed an order for a full set of knives which cost nearly a thousand dollars. She stated that the brand of cutlery that this salesman was selling was the brand her mother had owned, so even though she didn't need it, she very much wanted to own those knives.

As for the fourth reason on our list, well, perhaps some salespeople do manipulate prospects into buying, and "make" them buy something they otherwise would not have purchased, but we dismissed this kind of behavior back in Chapter Four as unacceptable. Besides, high pressure tactics are probably responsible for losing as many sales as they end up getting, and they reduce the persistency rate, which is the percentage of buyers who follow through with a purchase as opposed to those who cancel the order at a later time.

♦ The Real Reason People Buy ♦

You're probably wondering about the other 2% of people who did not answer with one of the four most popular responses. "How did *they* respond?" you may be thinking.

Not surprisingly, no more than one professional salesperson out of fifty gave what I believe is the true reason that people buy, and if you did Step Four in the last chapter, you realize that people will forgo their needs but they will move heaven and earth to get what they *want*. It is want that motivates people to buy. Whether they like you or not, or whether they trust you or not. Moreover, as we saw in the last chapter, they do not buy because of, but rather in spite of, their needs.

Want, however, is really a two sided coin.

People buy because they want what you are selling more than the *cost* of buying it. The cost being any combination of time, effort, money, risk, and reputation.

Alternatively, people buy because they want what you are selling more than they want to suffer the *consequences* of not having it.

In either case, the first five words of both of those statements are the same: People buy because they want. This means that, as a rule, people who want will buy, and people who do not want will not buy. I know this seems extremely elementary, but the truth really is that simple. Were it not, I would never have gone from failure to success in selling so quickly.

So if it really boils down to people wanting what you sell, it would seem that the key to selling is to figure out how to make them want it. How do you make prospects want what you are selling?

The answer is: You don't. Not at this stage, anyway.

No Objection Selling is designed around the psychology of the 21st century buyer who today is demanding a non-confrontational buying experience. If you take into account the condition of the prospect's mind, you will soon realize that before you ever make your first contact, your prospects have already been exposed to the best psychologically persuasive techniques money can buy.

◆ **Relentless Persuasion** ◆

Modern consumers are continuously being bombarded by TV and radio commercials, magazine and newspaper advertising, email and internet ads, as well as direct mail and telemarketing.

Then there is corporate sponsorship of sporting and other events, product placements in movies and TV shows, as well neuromarketing and subliminal techniques that you may not even be aware of. All of this is crafted by ad wizards and marketing gurus with PhDs in psychology who have studied reams of research data and conducted thousands of hours of focus groups. They know what works and why, and their companies have been spending millions of dollars per year to endlessly eat away at our resistance...relentlessly...right up to this moment.

If none of these psychological persuasion techniques have had an effect on your prospect, do you really think a few minutes of traditional sales talk from you to try to change their minds will make much difference at this point?

If so called "persuasive" closes, rebuttals and other sales techniques really worked, then why has there never been a book written by a sales guru who can show you how to successfully sell anything to anybody, *every time*?

Even the best salespeople often have closing ratios well below 50%. If you start counting from their initial contact, most are below 20%, and this is taking into account the fact that most salespeople are only calling on those who have already been qualified as prospective buyers, hence the term *prospect*.

The fact is, using persuasive techniques during a sales presentation will work to reinforce already held beliefs, but in most cases they will do little to change the minds of resistant skeptics.

♦ Integrated Selling ♦

There is a time and place for persuading, but it should start long before the sales appointment. For our purposes within this book, "selling" refers to the activities of the individual salespeople, which is tactical in nature. In properly designed sales organizations, however, persuading is a strategic function, and No Objection Selling should be implemented at the highest levels using an integrated selling system to optimize the persuasive power of the entire marketing arm of your company.

If you are an owner or executive officer of a sales organization, I encourage you to rethink your company's selling philosophy. Your salespeople are constantly on the front lines, interacting with your customers, and this places them in the ideal position for detecting any shifts in customer wants, and feeding that important intelligence back up the organization to the strategic decision makers.

On the other hand, if you are a sales person who does not have the authority to implement No Objection Selling at the highest levels of your company, there is good news! I initially applied it solely to my personal selling, and I was able to go from a failing sales rookie to the top producer among hundreds of seasoned sales professionals, with a closing ratio in excess of 98%, which means that virtually every time I set an appointment to talk with someone about their insurance, I made a sale. And those sales stuck, as evidenced by the fact that, over many years, I also achieved the company's highest client retention numbers.

♦ Why No Objection Selling Works ♦

No Objection Selling works at every level because it harmonizes with what 21st century buyers want. People want a non-confrontational buying experience, and you will get more sales, more referrals, and more repeat business if you commit to giving people what they want.

People buy what they want, and there are already plenty of people who want what you're selling, you just have to reach out to enough of them with your message on a favorable basis. A simple statement that makes this point well is the phrase, "Amateurs persuade, professionals sort."

This really sums up the No Objection Selling philosophy.

We will get into the details of exactly how to use this sorting approach to sell without overcoming objections, but if you realize that there are more than enough people out there right now who would gladly buy from you if you could just reach out to them on their terms, then you begin to understand that No Objection Selling is more about finding those people who are already persuaded. You just need a systematic, step-by-step, by-the-numbers way of finding them in a time efficient and cost effective manner.

Let's recap:

In Step One you refused to use rebuttals under any circumstances. You have dismissed the idea of handling objections forever.

Step Two involved determining in your mind that your prospect has to want what you're selling more than you want to take the trouble to sell it.

For Step Three you vowed never to treat conditions as objections.

Step Four involved memorizing the following: People will forgo their needs but they will move heaven and earth to get what they want.

At this point, you may already be envisioning how you can use these ideas to change your sales approach. If not, don't worry. It will all become crystal clear to you soon enough.

Step Five: Recognize that "Amateurs persuade, professionals sort." Believe this as it applies to your personal selling activities, and act accordingly.

Chapter Ten

♦

Prioritizing

How To Separate The Wheat From The Chaff

"Thanks to earpieces, it's getting harder to differentiate between schizophrenics and people talking on a cell phone."

Bob Newhart

If you will allow me, I'd like to engage your imagination for a moment.

Picture a football field on a beautiful summer day. Envision the way the bright white lines painted on the field contrast against the dark green turf as the sun shines down from the deep blue, cloudless sky overhead. Feel the gentle breeze as you study the field from the stands about twenty rows up, across from the fifty yard line.

You are alone in this stadium when suddenly people begin to appear on the field in front of you. Dozens, then several hundred people of all types appear, scattered randomly about the field. They are not doing anything in particular, just standing around. Some of them are old, while others are young. Some are large and sturdy while others are small or frail.

As you gaze upon this scene in front of you, you hear a voice. It tells you that during the next ten minutes you will be paid one thousand dollars for every person that you manage to get across the goal line on your left. You are not allowed to talk to them, and you have no weapons with which to threaten them to move. Your only method of getting them past the goal line is to push them, drag them, or pick them up and carry them across. Your time starts now.

It is doubtful that your first action would be to run straight ahead onto the middle of the field, find the biggest, meanest person thereabouts, and try to move him fifty yards to the goal line.

Most likely, if you have your senses about you, you would run as fast as you can to the goal line in question, find the smallest or frailest people standing on or near the line, and push them across. You would then seek out the next least resistant people closest to the goal line, and drag or carry them across also. Each time you successfully moved someone past the goal line, you would scan the field, mentally sorting the people, zeroing in on the easier subjects and then positioning them accordingly. If you happened upon someone who appeared to be an easy target but who put up much more resistance than expected, you would immediately leave that person and move on to the next.

This is how I would endeavor to accomplish this task, and I imagine it is how you would do it as well, because this is not a test of your ego, nor is about challenging one individual on the field. It is about positioning the maximum number of people across the goal line within the ten minute timeframe.

Although the act of pushing and dragging people is not a good behavior to carry over to selling, the idea of sorting your prospects is. This mental exercise clearly demonstrates the advantage of selectively prioritizing your prospects.

♦ Two Types of People ♦

If you subscribe to the No Objection Selling philosophy, then as far as selling is concerned, there are really only two types of people in your world.

The first are what I call *Non-buyers.*

Non-buyers are not going to buy. It does not matter what kind of closing technique you use on them, and it does not matter how many different rebuttals you come back with. For whatever their reasons, they are not buying. Hence the label: Non-buyers.

These people do not want what you are selling enough to make a buying commitment, and for them, nothing you say or do, within reason, will change their minds.

The traditional sales model would have you treat non-buyers as though they are buyers. You have probably heard that you should never prejudge a prospect as a non-buyer. While this is good advice, the alternative that traditional sells trainers and managers typically recommend is to treat all prospects as though they are buyers. But isn't that also prejudging?

For example, if a salesperson's closing ratio is thirty three percent, that means that he wastes two thirds of his time treating non-buyers as though they are buyers. Do lawyers treat non-clients as though they are clients? Do insurance companies treat non-insured people as though they are insured? Would a farmer spend two thirds of his time attempting to harvest where he had never sown?

Question: How much of *your* time do *you* wish to spend with non-buyers?

"None," is the answer I usually hear, and I agree. Ideally, we should spend no time with non-buyers, but as this is not always possible, I only wish to spend as little time as is necessary to *identify* them as non-buyers. How about you?

♦ Predisposed Buyers ♦

The other type of people in our world are those who are going to buy at some point in the near future, unless they are dissuaded by an objectionable salesperson. They may or may not buy now, but they will buy soon, and they may not necessarily buy from you, but they will buy from someone. We cannot call them buyers yet, but they are definitely not non-buyers, so I refer to them as *predisposed* buyers.

Predisposed buyers want what you are selling, or at least the benefits of what you are selling, and are persuaded or almost persuaded to buy. They will be giving someone their business soon, and if you can get in front of them on a favorable basis, you will probably make the sale.

Some of these predisposed buyers are already mentally prepared to buy, or close to it, and will buy immediately if you can just communicate to them that you have what they want. Others may need a little *soaking time.*

These two types of people, non-buyers and predisposed buyers, are very different from each other, and should be treated as such, so it is important to identify which type they are as quickly and inexpensively as possible.

People buy because they want. My definition of selling is simply finding people who want what I have, and then helping them get it.

Not everyone wants what you are selling, therefore not everyone will buy from you, so don't waste your efforts by treating everyone as though they are buyers. Remember, you are not a supplicant; you are someone who has the power to help people get what they want. People will move heaven and earth to get what they want, and you are in a position to help them! Value your time and be discriminate, because you have virtually no sway over people who do not want what you are selling, but you have tremendous power to serve those who do.

People who really want something will find a way to get it, and those who do not want it will resist any attempts to sell them. This is the rule. All rules have exceptions, but do you want to make your living depending on the few exceptions, or do you want to take advantage of the rule?

When you apply No Objection Selling, you are harmonizing with natural and psychological laws to tilt the playing field in your favor so you can sell consistently with far less effort.

◆ All Prospects Are Not Created Equal ◆

Another thing to consider is that when you are in front of a prospect, or have a prospect on the phone, the odds are against that person being the absolute best, most *mentally prepared to buy* prospect that you could be pitching at that moment. In fact, statistically, there is only a one in ten chance that this person is among the top

10% of prospects who are the most ready to buy now. Rather than treating all of your prospects as buyers, you're much better off identifying which type of prospect you are dealing with, and then prioritizing them accordingly before you pitch them.

Prioritizing prospects, rather than trying to sell someone just because you happen to have that person's ear, will save you much time and effort, and greatly increase your closing ratio.

Now, you may have already developed a good sorting system, one that allows you to choose which prospects rate your time and attention. If this is true, then you already have part of the No Objection Selling system working for you. You are one step closer to mastering No Objection Selling.

Some salespeople have the task of selling to walk-in customers. The key here is to create such a demand for your time that you literally need to work by appointment.

♦ Do not Attempt to Turn ♦ a No Into a Yes

My grandmother had an apple tree in her yard. In late summer, most of the apples would be small and hard, while a few of them were soft and sweet. Guess how much time I spent trying to talk a small, hard apple into being soft and sweet? You're right, I didn't. I ignored it and went for one that was ripe.

Earlier we mentioned the idea that "Amateurs persuade, professionals sort." In this vein, I wish to introduce another phrase that I recommend you adopt as one of your new standards for selling. It is the idea that, instead of trying to turn a no into a yes, look for more yeses.

Do not sell this idea short at first glance. the yeses are out there, if you seek them.

Rich DeVos is a billionaire and owner of the Orlando Magic professional basketball team. He began building his empire by selling vitamins, face to face. Here is what he said about trying to turn a no into a yes:

"People say yes or no for various reasons. Sometimes they can't afford it. Sometimes they don't want it. Sometimes they're not ready for it. It's a timing issue. And then you get back and you have a meeting and say, 'Well, if you would've done this…if you would've said that.' I say, forget all that and just go

find somebody else to talk to. So you've got to focus on just finding the people who are in tune with what you're doing at the right time. You've got to learn that everybody's not going to choose you, or your product, but if you tell it to enough people, you will sell."

You can approach people who do not want what you are selling, and because they are convenient, you can try to make them want it. Or you can look beyond the obvious and seek out people who want what you have, and sell it to them. The choice is yours.

If you seek, you will find. The yeses *are* out there, but you will not find them if you are busy trying to turn someone's no into a yes.

♦ An Offer They Can't Refuse ♦

Committing to seeking out yeses as opposed to trying to turn a no into a yes will not only change your selling paradigm and make it easier to close a sale, it also makes it easier to set an appointment with a prospect. For example, when setting a sales appointment, I inform my prospects that I use No Objection Selling exclusively, which means that I am not allowed to try to turn their no into a yes. I let them know that I *will* take no for an answer, and I ask them, "On that basis, can we get together?"

It is a hard offer to turn down if they have any desire to acquire the specialized information that an appointment with me will afford them, especially since telling them I will not try to turn a no into a yes is not just a selling tactic, it is a fact. Of course, if they do not want to learn more, then they are not qualified to merit my time, and I have no interest in meeting with them, so I welcome a no answer to that question as much as I would a yes. I recognize that I am not a supplicant, I am someone who has what people want, not just in terms of my product or service, but also in the non-confrontational behavior I treat them to throughout the process. I understand the extent to which they will go to get what they want, and I use this knowledge to serve them by helping them to get it.

Earlier, we spoke of sorting vs. persuading. This does not imply that we will not use persuasive techniques throughout the sales process. On the contrary, we use very powerful persuasive techniques during both the prospecting and selling phases.

I realize that this creates a dichotomy, because we are attempting to simultaneously lure in predisposed buyers with persuasion and screen out non-buyers by sorting. This is where the systematic No Objection Selling process really serves us. Creating a process that both attracts and repels the appropriate prospects removes the guesswork, and allows average and even below average salespeople to get above average results. And we must always do so in a courteous manner, because we never wish to burn bridges to future sales.

Using such a system, I was able to get far above average sales results, yet where skills, knowledge, and experience were concerned, I was, at that time, far below average.

They say that in the land of the blind, the one-eyed man is king. This idea points out that you do not have to be great to be better than the rest. All you have to do is find one thing that the others are *unwilling* to do, and you can differentiate yourself, and really stand out among your competitors.

Og Mandino once stated that you only have to be one step ahead of the crowd, and you are out in front. This again makes the point that being the best does not necessarily require greatness, just the willingness to go one step beyond what others are willing to do.

You've heard of the golden rule, which is to treat others the way you wish to be treated. But in selling, always apply the platinum rule, which is to treat prospects the way *they* wish to be treated. The difference can and often does make the sale.

♦ Commitment is Essential ♦

No Objection Selling works, but it requires a commitment to the principles and attitudes that we have previously discussed. You must truly commit for change to occur.

Step Six: Decide that you will no longer attempt to turn someone's no into a yes. Instead, commit to seeking out more yeses.

Chapter Eleven

♦

Quitting

You Don't Have To Close Every Time To Be Successful

"Coffee's for closers only!"

Alec Baldwin in the film *Glengarry Glen Ross*

One of the greatest salespeople of all time was a man by the name of Ben Feldman. In 1975 Mr. Feldman became the first man to sell $100 million worth of life insurance in one year. By the end of the 1970's, he was single-handedly selling more life insurance than 1,500 of the 1,800 insurance companies in the United States.

While some agents would use fear or shame in pushing a policy to a reluctant buyer, industry experts said Mr. Feldman would somehow discover a more positive approach that would harness a buyer's best instincts. Given Mr. Feldman's fantastic success, you would think that every sales organization would encourage their sales people to do the same. So why don't they?

One company, for example, was run by people who demanded that their sales reps set between twelve and fifteen appointments per week. To get in front of that many people week after week required meeting with anyone who would agree to an appointment, regardless of how unqualified a prospect they may have been. This involved using a very aggressive appointment setting approach, and not taking no for an answer.

But Philip Shields used a different approach. While the other sales reps scrambled to meet the weekly twelve-to-fifteen appointment quota, Phil usually only set between four and six appointments, closed between 80% and 100% of them, and as a result, consistently outproduced all of the other sales reps in his region, placing Phil among the very top producers nationally in his organization.

This top achiever knew something that the other sales reps and even the management did not understand. Phil realized that sales are not made by wasting time with non-buyers. He also knew that success in sales comes from knowing when to take no for an answer. Sorting, rather than persuading, was Phil's key to consistently remaining among the top sales producers in his company, which just happened to be the leader in its industry in the United States.

♦ Instant Improvement ♦

In an earlier chapter, you read about W. Clement Stone, the billionaire insurance pioneer who created the world's largest insurance brokerage firm.

While he was still in high school, W. Clement Stone began working for his mother's accident insurance agency in Detroit. She instructed him to introduce himself to business people and try to sell everyone he approached. So he followed her instructions, and sold two policies his first day. The second day, he sold four policies. On his third day, he sold six policies.

On the fourth day, he learned an important lesson, the effect of which resulted in the young W. Clement Stone selling twenty seven policies that day.

The lesson? Simply this: Do not to waste precious time trying to sell a non-buyer. This simple principle eventually helped him to build an insurance empire that spans the globe.

Here is another way of phrasing this important lesson, as stated by Mr. Stone himself: "Know when to quit."

When he started out, he was instructed to try to sell everyone he called on, so he stayed with every prospect. Sometimes he wore them out, but in making the sale, he became worn out also.

As a result, he decided not to try to sell everyone he called on if the sale would take longer than a time limit that he set for himself. His new goal, as he put it, was to, "Make the prospect happy and leave quickly," because, "fatigue is not conducive to doing your best work."

Immediately he increased his average sales per day tremendously.

It is true that had he stayed with every prospect he would have undoubtedly sold some of the ones he gave up on, but that would have taken more time, which would have resulted in fewer overall sales. Besides, his mother was not paying him extra for difficult sales, every sale paid the same. Nor was he paid per rebuttal, so the extra effort of overcoming objections would have provided no gain, and would only have cost him time, effort, money, and reputation.

Also, Mr. Stone soon discovered that when he was ready to move on to his next prospect, the difficult prospects could see that he was not desperate to make the sale, and not willing to be objectionable by trying to wear them down, and he stated that many times they would ask him to come back and sell them a policy.

♦ The Benefits of Quitting ♦

No Objection Selling takes advantage of knowing when to quit, and the result is a completely non-confrontational approach that empowers salespeople to sell without ever having to deal with sales objections. This works for two reasons:

Firstly, it allows you to reach more pre-disposed buyers in less time, and as sales is a numbers game, this results in more sales.

Secondly, modern consumers prefer it, and in most cases they are demanding it!

I realize that the concept of knowing when to quit, and not trying to sell every prospect, may seem like a cop-out to people steeped in the overcoming objection mentality. Thanks to years of indoctrination in the traditional sales model, many of the ideas and concepts of No Objection Selling do not make sense to people who have bought into the conventional way of selling. Sometimes, however, different ways of doing things, which initially seem wrong, are often correct. For example:

A grocer put up a sign in his window that read:

Eggplants: 25¢ Each / Three for $1.00

All day long, customers came in exclaiming: "Don't be ridiculous! I should get *four* for a dollar!"

Meekly the grocer would capitulate and package four eggplants.

The tailor next door had been watching these antics and finally asked the grocer, "Aren't you going to fix the mistake on your sign?"

"What mistake?" the grocer asked, "Before I put up that sign no one ever bought more than one eggplant."

♦ Never Give In? ♦

I have a saying that I repeat often to myself. It is the phrase, "Never give in!" It comes from the famous speech given by Sir Winston Churchill where he advised his audience to "Never give in, except to convictions of honor and good sense."

Often in sales, people adopt the never give in mentality, bent on making every effort to turn a no into a yes to get the sale. These people are unaware that this approach lacks honor and does not make good sense, so they continue to perpetuate the poor reputation of the sales profession by "leaving a trail of bodies in their wake." Yet they still feel justified in their methods, purely based on their misunderstanding of the never give in philosophy.

To me, never giving in does not mean to be objectionable to decent people simply because I am trying to get their money. Rather, it means to never stop searching for a better way. Circumstances change, technology advances, and people move on to new and different wants. We must always be searching for a better way and be willing to quit an action or change a behavior if it is not getting us the desired results.

One of the lessons I have learned from the game of baseball is that you don't have to bat a thousand to be successful. In fact, any batter who can hit safely three times out of ten consistently can pretty much name his salary.

You can also benefit from these ideas. Determine in your mind to know when to quit. Identify an appropriate maximum amount of time and effort you are willing to invest in a prospect before you move on, and do so without burning bridges. Factor this timeframe into your sales approach, and develop a system around it.

Step Seven: Set a specific amount of time that you are willing to spend with a prospect before moving on to the next one. Know when to quit.

Chapter Twelve

♦

Problems

Sell Them On The Problem And They Will Demand The Solution

Customer: "I want to return this product I purchased from you."

Salesperson: "We don't sell products, we sell solutions."

Customer: "After trying your solution, I've decided that I want my problem back."

Which statement would more likely motivate you to want to buy a new fan belt for your car?

1) A brand new fan belt will last a long time and run more quietly than your current one.

2) Your old fan belt could break at any moment, leaving you stranded on the road, possibly many miles from assistance.

The first statement is an example of selling the benefits. The second statement is an example of selling the problem.

Selling the problem is an axiom, and is so important to successful selling that I have included a chapter on this very conventional yet vital concept in an otherwise unconventional book.

Sometimes selling the problem is not necessary, however, when it is appropriate, it is the most powerful way to help the prospect want what you are selling and motivate them to commit to taking action now.

This is because, as we explored the two sides of why people buy in Chapter Nine, we identified one of those sides as wanting to buy more than suffering the consequences of not buying.

People take action either because they wish to move towards pleasure, or because they want to move away from pain. More often than not, moving away from pain is the motivator most people choose to dictate their actions.

We do not use fear or negativity as a weapon against such people, as that would not be in their best interest. Benjamin Disraeli stated, "Next to knowing when to seize an opportunity, the most important thing in life is to know when to forgo an advantage."

Instead, we truthfully and accurately present the downside to not buying what we are selling so they can gain the proper perspective and make an informed decision. Carefully sell the problem with restraint. Endeavor to not go overboard as one life insurance salesperson did:

> **"Don't let me frighten you into a decision. Sleep on it tonight, and *if* you wake up in the morning, let me know what you think."**

◆ A Safe Trip? ◆

Let's expand on the fan belt idea for a moment. My wife's mother often travels to the other side of the state to visit relatives. If the person who changes her vehicle's oil was to notice that the fan belt was old and cracked, it is unlikely that he would sell her on spending the extra money to have a new one installed by using the first statement in our previous example, because she doesn't necessarily want a longer lasting, quieter running fan belt.

On the other hand, it is likely that the second statement would appeal to what she wants, which is to avoid becoming stranded miles from help. And being the wonderful son-in-law that I am, I would want the serviceman to do his best to make her aware of the situation so she would want to resolve it, for her safety and convenience.

Which approach would you want the serviceman to take if someone you cared about was depending upon that vehicle to function properly?

Of course, he had better be telling the truth, and not exaggerating the peril just to make a sale. We have probably all experienced this. Many years ago my vehicle was getting a simple oil change, and the mechanic tried to get me to spring for an extra $700 for something that was, in my opinion, completely unnecessary. He tried to scare me by telling me that my vehicle would not make it another week without the extra work. More than five years later, I finally traded that vehicle in for a newer one, and in all that time, the problems he promised never materialized.

The risk involved in buying something is always on the minds of buyers, but the risk of not buying is also important. To demonstrate to your prospect that you care about what he or she cares about, both of these concerns should be addressed when selling. People want to buy from someone they believe understands their problems, and cares about helping solve them.

♦ The Physician's Selling Method ♦

Here is another example of how selling the problem makes it easier to close the sale:

Imagine that after examining you, your doctor gave you a prescription and told you that this awful tasting liquid would cost $100 per week, make you feel horrible, and that you should take it six times per day for six months. I can just imagine the resistance you would probably put up. You would want to know what is in the stuff and why your doctor wants you to take it, wouldn't you? If your doctor just left it at that, it isn't very likely that you would want to get that prescription filled, is it?

On the other hand, if your doctor instead finished the examination and then began explaining that you have a problem, and began showing you x-rays and printouts of blood tests, and explained that this problem will result in your premature death in very short order, your attitude would be somewhat different, wouldn't it?

Moreover, when you were informed that the cure to save your life would *only* cost $100 a week for six months, you would be begging your doctor to write out your prescription, wouldn't you?

Selling the problem provides a completely different perspective, doesn't it?

♦ What is High Pressure Selling? ♦

Most people who do not sell for a living consider the traditional sales model to be high pressure selling, however, the idea of high pressure is quite relative. Different people perceive pressure differently. I define high pressure as: Using, misusing, or failing to use sales techniques that cause the prospect to feel uncomfortable with me.

Notice that I included *failing to use* sales techniques as a contributor to high pressure. This is because, as the professional in the relationship, we have a duty to exhibit certain behavior towards the prospect. We must use various selling techniques to cater to prospects and make them feel comfortable with us. For example, we must apply professional listening skills and focus on the prospect's wants. If we fail to work at developing the relationship, we will have failed the prospect, because ours is the servant's role; we do not expect the prospect to do the same for us.

Another technique or skill that we as sales professionals ought to be using is style awareness, or behavior mirroring. These techniques, which are well documented and discussed in many traditional sales books, help the salesperson to be more cognizant of the buyer's style so as to avoid the "landmine" of acting in a manner that causes discomfort for the prospect.

Notice also that I define high pressure as discomfort towards *me*. I have no problem with making the prospect uncomfortable, as long as the source of that discomfort is their realization of what will happen if they fail to take action to solve their problem. After all, the thought of suffering the consequences of not buying is often the *only* reason people are motivated to take action in the first place.

When appealing to what a prospect wants, it is appropriate to discuss the consequences of not buying. Keep it accurate, and present the facts as you see them. If your prospect does not want to solve the problem, then they can turn down your offer. That is fine, we are not afraid nor ashamed of taking no for an answer.

Sell the problem rather than the benefits, because when prospects buy into the problem, they will demand the solution. Quoting the late, great Ben Feldman, "If you can show them that it will cost them more not to buy than to buy, they will buy."

Step Eight: Determine not to sell your prospects on features or benefits. Sell them on the problem, and they will demand the solution.

Chapter Thirteen

♦

Prospecting

The Difference Between Prospecting And Selling

Prospecting is as different from selling as a prospect is different from a sale.

Do you know the difference between prospecting and selling?

Obviously, selling something results in a commission, whereas obtaining a prospect does not. But you cannot make a sale until you have a prospect, can you?

I am amazed at how few leaders of sales organizations appreciate the differences between prospecting and selling.

Prospecting requires someone with a certain frame of mind and skill set to make dozens or hundreds of initial contacts with suspects each day, and then successfully sort them properly. Prospecting must be done repeatedly, day in and day out. You cannot let up, because you cannot make sales if you have no prospects to call on.

Prospecting is mundane drudgery, but you need prospects to start the sales process.

Selling, on the other hand, is creative and dynamic. Interacting with qualified prospects to identify their wants and mesh them with what you have, identifying their problems and presenting your information in a captivating manner, and then getting the order and settling the details, all require the type of abilities that are more commonly associated with the successful salesperson.

Far too many sales organizations, however, expect one individual to fulfill both functions successfully. Trying to find one person who possesses the talents and skills to both prospect and sell successfully has always been a major hurtle to building a sales force. In fact, I believe this is one of the biggest reasons for the horrible churn in the selling profession; expecting one person to develop two diametrically opposed skill sets.

Even if a single individual can accomplish both functions, they usually hate the one or dread the other, and as such are not as effective nor as efficient as they would be if they only had to focus on the one component for which they are best suited.

If you are depending upon a successful "seller" to do your prospecting, you are not optimizing your resources, and your results are suffering. You have put a square peg into a round hole.

Similarly, if you send a successful "prospector" out to close deals for you, you may be losing some of the sales you really should be getting.

If you wish to successfully integrate your sales activities for maximum effect, start by dividing up your sales force into prospecting and selling departments, even going so far as to give them separate leadership. Just as advertising and public relations are completely different functions that work towards a common cause, prospecting and selling are also different, although they are both essential to getting sales.

If you are a salesperson, hire and train someone who is ideally suited to the drudgery of contacting strangers and sorting them for hours at a time. If you cannot afford to do this, don't feel bad, because when I first started out, I could not afford to hire anyone either, so instead I became two people.

♦ What Worked For Me ♦

When I was in the prospecting mode, I intentionally turned off every "sales" instinct. I scheduled time specifically for prospecting, and I didn't let anything get in the way of it. I resisted every temptation to sell to anyone, and instead stuck to my prospecting script. No matter how interested they appeared to be, I prospected and sorted.

When I was in the selling mode, I spent no time with non-qualified suspects. I stayed the course and kept the prospecting and selling functions completely separate.

Because I used No Objection Selling for both, I did not hate either of them, but I do prefer getting out and pitching people and closing deals considerably more than making hundreds of cold calls to strangers. That is just me, however. We are all different.

My early prospecting consisted of contacting people from the phone book or a street directory. As there was no possible way to cross-reference these names against a company client list, I had no way of knowing whether the person on the other end of the line was insured with my company. If they were, I was not permitted to sell to them, so I needed a quick way to sort them.

I did this by creating a short script that quickly identified who I was, what company I represented, what I was selling, what their problem might be, and how I could possibly help them solve it. This was stated in such a way so as to gain their favorable attention. I would then ask if they were already insured with my company. All of this took about 20 seconds. If they said yes, I politely apologized and ended the call. Of course, the answer I wanted to hear was no.

Up until that time, I had always been told to get the prospect saying yes and keep them saying yes. What I was doing went against that rule, but interestingly, I discovered that after these prospects got their no out of the way, they seemed much more amenable to listening to the rest of my script and going along with it. That is when I realized that pretty much everyone has a no inside waiting to come out the instant he or she recognizes that you are a salesperson trying to sell something. If you get them saying yes, they will not have the opportunity to let the no out, and the negativity seems to build up, like steam under pressure. Giving them an opportunity to release their no seems to make the process go easier.

♦ The Importance of Perceived Control ♦

Later I discovered that part of the reason No Objection Selling works so well is due to the control the prospects perceive that they have over the buying process. Buyers do not mind professional guidance, but if they perceive manipulation of any kind, which they find objectionable, they will naturally object.

Many traditional salespeople believe that they must ask questions to control the sale. The reality is, they are controlling the conversation, but the buyer is always in control of the sale. Attempting to take control of or manipulate someone's will to cause them to buy only works with a small segment of the population. The rest will object to such behavior, and rightly so.

The perception of one's control over a situation is a very powerful factor in determining how a person behaves. Tom Peters, the world-renowned business consultant and author of the bestselling book *In Search of Excellence*, reported on a study where people of all types sat in a room and were asked to proofread for errors as well as solve puzzles. As they worked, the sounds of street noise, a mimeograph machine, a person speaking Armenian, and other sounds were piped into the room. The assumption was that this jumble of noises would hinder the subject's ability to concentrate, which would reduce the number of errors they would catch, and the number of puzzles they could solve.

As a control, half of the people were given a button that, when pressed, would mute the noise. Not surprisingly, the subjects who had the buttons solved twice as many puzzles, and caught three times as many proofreading errors.

What was surprising was that in not one instance did any of those people actually press their button! The mere perception that they had control over their situation resulted in a dramatic increase in both their performance and their productivity.

The more control people believe they have, the less stressed they tend to be. Proof of this exists in casinos all over the USA, where more and more gambling space is being reconfigured from table games to slot machines and video games because studies have revealed that most gamblers prefer not to have dealers or other players interacting with them. The players perceive more control and better enjoy gambling when these elements are removed from the equation and replaced with a non-confrontational experience.

♦ A Second Chance ♦

Getting back to the prospecting script. If the prospect's answer to my initial question was "no," meaning they were not currently insured by my company and thus fair game for me to try to win their business, then I would ask them if they would like me to send them information so they can discover if they are currently overpaying or missing out on some valuable benefits by not being insured by my company.

Note that I was not trying to sell them on the benefits of buying from me, but rather I was selling them on the problem of not knowing which benefits they were missing out on and how much it was costing them, while offering to solve that problem for the cost of answering a few brief questions.

Additionally, notice that I was not attempting to lead them, I was instead carefully screening them by asking a second qualifying question to solicit their cooperation in taking them to the next step, this time seeking a *yes* response.

Unfortunately, we do not always receive acceptance at this point, even from pre-disposed buyers, because they usually have not had adequate time to absorb what is really being offered. They may still be processing the fact that we are not a friend, a relative, or some other important person known to them. Their defenses tend to go up as this realization occurs.

Because of this, if they fail to demonstrate a positive response, I always give them a second chance. It is really a *last* chance, at least for now. I rephrase my last statement and ask my qualifying question for a second and final time.

Often, many people who say no or otherwise indicate a negative response the first time will reconsider and answer in the affirmative the second time, not because I am being forceful or persistent, but because during the initial moments of a prospecting contact, people just don't seem to immediately grasp how you are offering to serve them. Notice, however, that simply rephrasing the question one final time is the *only* behavior I would offer to a negative response.

If their response to my second and final attempt is also negative, I thank them kindly and hang up, leaving them with the understanding that I *will* take no for an answer. This will serve me when I contact them again in the future to see if their wants have changed.

As you can see, my only pitch in the initial prospecting phase was to offer information that would appeal to the prospect's curiosity. I offered them an opportunity to discover if they were receiving less than they could, or paying more than they should. I never mentioned switching their insurance companies. Curiosity compelled people who were perfectly happy with their current companies to give me the three or four minutes of their time I needed to obtain enough information to put together an estimate quote.

To prospect effectively, offer one compelling benefit, such as a price quote or other valuable information. If they have no interest in this benefit, move on. You'll discover that when you come back the next time, you will be received more readily due to your non-confrontational approach.

In the years since I left the insurance business, we have successfully utilized variations of this approach for our clients in just about every type of business that has something to sell.

♦ Prospecting is not Selling ♦

Think for a moment about a person who literally prospects for gold. You realize that they are not attempting to *transform* dirt or rock into gold, they are moving the dirt and rock to *get* to the gold. Often, several tons of earth and rock must be moved to acquire a single ounce of gold.

Effective prospecting for customers necessitates spending no time trying to turn a no into a yes, but rather, you quickly sort through the no's to get to the yeses.

The very important protocol for prospecting is to remember that your goal is not to attempt to *sell* your product or service, it is to move the qualified prospects to the next phase of the sales process, or screen them out and dismiss them.

◆ Prospecting Among Businesses ◆

When setting initial face-to-face appointments with decision makers of businesses, one way to screen out non-buyers *and* attract predisposed buyers is to offer an educational "executive briefing" that provides useful information that will benefit the prospect whether they buy or not. This allows you to better choose with whom you wish to invest your time.

For an even more powerful hook, offer a briefing that contains ideas for helping your prospects increase their revenue or create a new revenue stream. This appeals to pretty much every businessperson, and it allows you to not just *find* a customer, but you can actually *create* a customer with this approach. When Ted Levitt redefined the purpose of a corporation as that of "creating a customer," I don't believe that he intended to exclude the sales department, or even individual sales reps, from this purpose. Creating value for the customer rather than just communicating the value of your product or service will allow you as a salesperson to greatly increase your total solution package and, as a result, increase your prospect's desire to buy from you.

♦ Don't be Fooled by "Hot" Prospects ♦

One of the biggest mistakes I have observed salespeople make in their prospecting is when they mistakenly believe that because someone needs what they are selling so very badly, they are the perfect candidate to buy it. They prioritize this person as a hot lead, and then they, or the "closer" if the lead is handed off, will go to great lengths to try to convince this person that their product will solve the problem that is plaguing them so badly, but to no avail. Often, what the salesperson believes to be the "perfect" prospect turns out to be a non-buyer.

Why is this? Quite simply, the sales person was looking at the prospect's need rather than the prospect's want. If you think about it, if the prospect had wanted to solve that problem, he most likely would have solved it long before it became so significant. The very fact that this person needed the product so badly indicated that he was not a very good candidate for the salesperson to pitch.

On the other hand, the best prospects tend to be those people who do not need the product because they solved the problem with a previous purchase. They do not need your product, but they may want it, and if there is any way you can go in with a newer version or a similar product with some other advantage, they may be very open to the idea of buying.

Remember that the best prospect is, and always will be, a satisfied customer. Even someone who is satisfied with a product they bought from your competitor can be a great prospect for you, because you know that they value the kind of product or service that you sell as evidenced by the fact that they bought it in the past.

◆ Do Not Attract Non-Buyers ◆

Another mistake I have observed often concerning prospecting is when sales people tailor their prospecting script to appeal to non-buyers. Do not give non-buyers one ounce of consideration when crafting your script! No matter how well you try to entice them, or how compelling your pitch may be, they will not buy, but by being attractive to them, you will draw them in and waste your time with them.

I wish I had a dollar for every time I have observed a salesperson complain about the "garbage" leads the telemarketing department had given to them. Sending a salesperson out to waste their time on a non-buyer does nothing to foster trust and harmony within a sales force, and as a result, everyone pays the price.

Always use the prospecting script as a way of screening out non-buyers. Keep in mind that if someone does not want to give you a few minutes of their attention, it is doubtful that they will give you their money.

♦ Walk-In Situations ♦

I believe that a sales professional should strive to work exclusively by appointment as much as possible. This becomes more challenging when you are dependent upon walk-in prospects to keep you busy.

There are many books on how to drive traffic to your retail location using internet marketing, direct mail, print ads, special events, and more. These approaches have their plusses and minuses, and as they are not exclusive to No Objection Selling, I will leave it to you to decide which ones work best for your situation.

♦ Getting Past the Gatekeeper ♦

I do wish to mention briefly one area of prospecting that seems to be the target of a lot of wrong information. It is the concept of getting past the gatekeeper.

I am rather appalled by the number of experts who advise either lying by stating that the person you are trying to reach knows you and is expecting your call, lying by stating that you are someone you are not, or attempting to bully or confuse the gatekeeper. Another tactic is to so badger the gatekeeper that his or her boss–your prospect–finally steps in, and now you have your prospect's ear, but not on a very favorable basis! These tactics once again prove the levels to which people will lower themselves when the possibility of acquiring money is involved.

CEOs, especially those of large corporations, do not hire high school interns to be their executive assistants. They hire sophisticated, experienced business people, and often pay them salaries upwards of six figures. In almost all cases you are not going to bully your way past them. Additionally, many smaller company CEOs may put their spouse or child or another relative in the position of gatekeeper. Try to run roughshod over him or her, and you will *not* be getting any of that company's business anytime soon.

I have spent the past 15 years selling directly to company owners, presidents and CEOs, and I do not pretend to be the expert on getting through to all of them, but any approach that lacks professional courtesy and honesty is unacceptable in my book.

If it's a CEO of a large corporation you're after, the gatekeeper may actually be the person with whom you will want to set the initial appointment. This could also save you a lot of wasted time, as the gatekeeper may be able to direct you to a more appropriate decision maker within the company for what you are selling. Having the CEO's executive assistant on your side can't hurt, can it?

My personal method for reaching business leaders, even for some smaller companies, has always been to specifically ask for my prospect's executive assistant and seek their support and assistance first. They have helped me far more often than they have hindered me.

The most important thing to remember is to appeal to a person's want. Why would the gatekeeper want to assist you in securing time with his or her boss? Why would the big boss want to give you any time?

Remember that prospecting is as different from selling as a prospect is different from a sale. Think of ways that you can separate your prospecting from your selling. For example, if you have ten salespeople, maybe what you really need are seven prospectors and three sales people.

Step Nine: Find a way to separate your prospecting from your selling, and determine to keep them separate.

Chapter Fourteen

♦

Process

A System For Selling Without Dealing With Objections

> *"You can take great people, highly trained and motivated, and put them in a lousy system and the system will win every time."*
>
> **Geary Rummler, CEO, Performance Design Lab**

"I just wanted to make a decision and get out of there!"

This attitude is common when dealing with a persistent sales rep whose goal is to get your money.

It shouldn't be, however, because people usually enjoy buying things. Either they are excited to acquire their new purchase, or, even if they are buying an insurance policy or making a purchase for their business, they are happy to have the decision behind them. Purchasing a product or service is usually not such a bad experience. On the other hand, enduring a salesperson prior to and even after the purchase is often a less than pleasurable time for buyers.

Take Terence Hockenhull, for instance. Terry is the President of Charteris, Inc., a training and consulting firm located in Southeast Asia.

Some years ago, Terry had to purchase a fax machine for his company. This was back when fax machines were very expensive and the selection was far more limited than it is today. Terry invited a number of companies to compete for the order.

One salesman spent 20 minutes trying to push a machine that Terry felt was inferior and inadequate. Another salesman, whom Terry knew socially, tried to get him to buy based on friendship.

The third salesman took the time to find out how Terry intended to use the machine. He asked if Terry would be faxing internationally, whether single page or multiple page messages were more common, if he would be faxing to the same parties on a regular basis, etc.

Only after the salesman had gathered the answers to these and other questions did he recommend a model with a multiple page document tray, a stored number feature, and delayed transmission. He then carefully explained how the features of his model would save Terry both time and money.

His fax machine was by no means the cheapest, but Terry bought it with no regrets.

Now for the rest of the story ...

Both of the other salesmen had machines that offered the same features as the one Terry selected, and one of the models was significantly less expensive than the one Terry bought. While two of the salesmen were concerned about what *they* wanted, however, one salesman was concerned about what Terry wanted.

The bottom line is Terry wanted to buy from the third salesman, not because they were friends, not because of price, but because Terry felt that this salesman cared about helping him solve his problem, and this factored into that salesman's total solution package. This is the kind of buying experience that prospects are looking for, and are even willing to pay extra for.

Can they count on you to give it to them?

This example really represents what is referred to as "Consultative Selling" which is by no means exclusive to the No

Objection Selling approach, nor is it necessarily a pattern for the No Objection Selling process. This example simply serves to make the point that people buy based on their wants, and discovering what they really want and giving it to them will make for easier selling for the salesperson and a better buying experience for the customer.

It is true that people like to buy, but they usually do not like to be sold. Far too many sales situations involve an unpleasant experience for the prospects and customers, where salespeople place landmines in the way of the sale in the form of objectionable behavior, making it more difficult and less desirable for the prospect to buy.

The public is demanding non-confrontational buying experiences, and they will turn to kiosks, the internet, and even their cell phones to get what they want. It is time for salespeople to make it a priority to give the public an easy, helpful, and pleasant buying experience every time.

Some experts believe that customers are calling for the elimination of all human interaction in the buying process wherever possible. While it is true that this trend is on the rise, I do not believe the reason is because buyers don't want to deal with salespeople. Instead, I believe it is because customers don't want to deal with *objectionable* salespeople. And while technology allows more products and services to now be purchased without human assistance, the fact remains that with the proliferation of high tech purchasing opportunities comes a countering desire for "high touch" to balance things out. People still need people, as Barbara Streisand pointed out, but they need helpful, considerate, servant-minded people rather than objectionable, high pressure salespeople.

In fact, the public would be more likely to seek out sales professionals, and become more open to welcoming them into their homes and businesses if they knew that they would not have to endure an unpleasant buying experience. As we discussed in Chapter Ten, informing prospects of your non-confrontational methods for the purpose of more easily securing an appointment is one of the many benefits of committing to the No Objection Selling approach.

◆ Good Sales Ideas are Enhanced ◆ by No Objection Selling

It is not uncommon for traditional sales people to have many good ideas and techniques. Occasionally, if these techniques are applied properly and with skill, there may never come a point in the sale where rebuttals need to be brought out. The prospect may easily make the buying commitment and then all that is left is to settle the details.

One of the many good concepts often utilized by successful salespeople is the idea of positioning yourself as an "assistant buyer." This is where you try to get on the same side of the table as your prospect, so he or she will view you as a trusted advisor. Some people refer to this as consultative selling. This is a good strategy, but unless you adopt the No Objection Selling philosophy, you may fall into the trap of succumbing to the traditional method of bantering back and forth with the prospects that you are supposed to be assisting, rebutting their objections, and losing credibility as their advocate.

The difference between No Objection Selling and a traditional soft sell is that we have determined that we will not fall back on the rebuttal approach under any circumstances. We don't "sell the need" but instead focus on what the prospect wants. We will not attempt to close a deal until we know that the prospect wants to buy, and we do not try to convince a prospect to buy something he or she does not want or is not mentally prepared to buy. As the old saying goes, "A man convinced against his will is of the same opinion still."

Remember, the public wants a non-confrontational buying experience. If you give it to them, they will prefer to buy from you. You may lose a sale here or there that a skilled, high pressure persuader might have gotten, but you will be writing up so many more deals, so much more easily, that your overall results will be better, and your customers will be happier. This also creates more opportunities for referrals and repeat business.

♦ Do Not Burn Bridges ♦

Sometimes people are not ready to buy, perhaps because, among other reasons, you simply do not have the best deal for them, and it just does not make good business sense for them to buy from you at that time. I often sold to people months or even years after my initial contact when their circumstances had changed, and they cited my non-confrontational approach as the main reason for coming back to me and eventually becoming my customer.

In fact, the most referrals I ever received from one person were sent to me by someone who was not even my client! When I tried to get his business, I just could not come close to the fantastic deal he was getting from his wife's employer, but he so appreciated my No Objection Selling approach that he referred more business to me than any other single source. Several years later, he divorced, and as he no longer qualified for his ex-wife's deal, he immediately came to me without doing any comparison-shopping. After all those years of referring his friends, relatives, neighbors and co-workers, he was finally able to join them in becoming my client!

♦ The Traditional Model vs. ♦ No Objection Selling

In the traditional sales model, the process tends to flow from fact finding–often called needs analysis–to developing and offering up a solution, to discussing the benefits of the solution, to the close, which rarely happens without resistance in the form of objections. These are then countered with rebuttals until the sale is finally won or lost. Some proprietary sales methods may diverge slightly from this process, but in general, this is how the sale progresses.

Traditional Sales Model

♦ The No Objection Selling Process ♦

No Objection Selling begins with attempting to discover what the prospect really wants. It is this want that drives the sale. Nothing matters unless it appeals to the prospect's want. This then leads to the phase where the problems keeping the prospect from getting what he or she wants, as well as the problems inherent in not buying from you, are revealed and discussed. With No Objection Selling, we often sell them on their problem, because once they buy into the problem, they will demand the solution.

Next, the prospect's conditions must be ascertained and negotiated. We do not confuse the conditions with objections because at this point we have not attempted to close the deal, so we are not trying to get a decision yet. Instead, we have opened the door to the prospect's input on conditions or specifications. We are not countering or rebutting their demands, we are exploring together with the prospect a solid understanding of what they want and what they are willing to do to get it.

Next, if we can give the prospect what they want, we reveal a solution that satisfies their want, and then we settle the details.

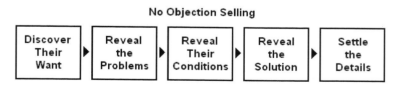

Notice that the boxes state that we *reveal* the problems, and we *reveal* the solution. The more you are able to guide the prospects into discovering these things for themselves, the more readily they will accept them without resistance.

One way of doing this without being objectionable is to ask for the prospect's opinion. People are always happy to offer their opinions, and this behavior is preferable to confronting them with a demand for a decision, something to which they might easily object.

For a moment, I would like you to think as a buyer rather than a seller. Looking at the following two flow charts, ask yourself which one you would like a salesperson to follow when helping you to buy something:

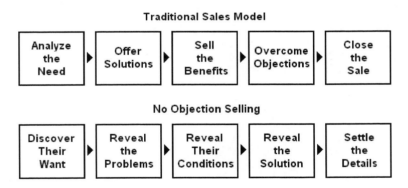

As mentioned earlier, in addition to talking about the problems our product or service will solve, we also explore with our prospects the problems inherent in buying from us. One such problem is the money they have to pay, another is risk, another might be the amount of time to learn to use the new product, etc. These problems could all become points of resistance if we wait until the close, because they are always on our prospect's minds, possibly foremost on their minds, and to ignore them is to ignore the problems of the person we supposedly are there to assist. Doing so would indeed be objectionable behavior on our part.

One good technique to help uncover a genuine concern they may have expressed about your product or service is to "peel back the onion" by asking, "Is that your only reason?" or "In addition to that, would there be any other reason?" Many traditional salespeople use this technique for getting to the real objection. The technique is a good one, but my motive is not to get to an objection, but rather to help the buyer explore, and the seller learn, what the prospect really wants and why. This is not a matter of semantics because the buyer's true thoughts about what they want is not an objection, it is not even a point of resistance, it is simply a condition, and we have discussed the differences between objections and conditions.

♦ Always Confirm the Buying Decision ♦

When you believe that the prospect is ready to buy, you must confirm their decision to become your customer before you treat them as such. I believe in confirming by simply asking them a question, which is usually a form of the following:

"If you want it, and you can easily afford it, why not give it a try?"

I use the word try rather than buy because virtually no initial purchase decision is a permanent commitment, and trying implies less risk than buying.

If I were selling a new car, I would reform the question to appeal to the prospect's most important want. If it was safety, I might ask, "If you want this kind of protection for yourself and your family, and you can easily afford it, why not give it a try?"

If I were selling advertising, I might ask, "If you believe that this can outperform your last campaign, and you can easily afford it, why not give it a try?"

An even simpler way to confirm their purchase decision is simply to ask, "Is this the one you want?"

◆ The No Objection Selling Advantage ◆

Ultimately, you will come to an agreement with your prospect regarding exactly what you can offer and what it will cost. This, along with the non-confrontational sales method employed, will combine to create a total solution package. If the prospect wants your solution package more than he or she wants your competitor's, then you will get the sale. If you do not have what the prospect wants, take no for an answer and move on, letting them know that you will be there for them if their wants or their circumstances change. You will be surprised how often the prospect will choose No Objection Selling even though the competitor's price or product may appear to be more favorable. I have seen this happen time and again when working with clients who offer a wide range of products and services within many different industries.

If you can differentiate yourself by the *way* you sell your product or service, you will have gained a tremendous advantage over your competition. Salespeople have sold their products and services as a direct result of using the No Objection Selling approach, even though their price was higher or their competitor's product had some other advantage. Do not under-estimate the positive impact No Objection Selling can have. You are giving the public a buying experience that they want.

To summarize, the No Objection Selling system culminates in a different result–an easy sale–far more often than traditional selling does because it uses a different process, backed by different motives. The prospect more readily perceives that we understand their problems and we want to help them solve those problems because our approach is non-confrontational.

Step Ten: Commit to treating your prospects to a non-confrontational buying experience by using the No Objection Selling process below:

1) **Discover Their Want**
2) **Reveal the Problems**
3) **Reveal Their Conditions**
4) **Reveal the Solution**
5) **Settle the Details**

On the following page you will find a list of all ten steps, which are also the ten key components of No Objection Selling.

The Ten Key Components
of No Objection Selling

1) Reject, without exception, the traditional selling tactic of attempting to overcome sales objections with rebuttals.

2) Decide that prospects have to want what you're selling more than you want to take the trouble to sell it.

3) Commit to never treating a condition as an objection. Always identify a prospect's conditions and negotiate a satisfactory settlement before you attempt to close.

4) Determine never again to sell the need. Realize that people will forgo their needs but they will move heaven and earth to get what they want.

5) Recognize that "Amateurs persuade, professionals sort." Believe this as it applies to your personal selling activities, and act accordingly.

6) Decide that you will no longer attempt to turn someone's no into a yes. Instead, commit to seeking out more yeses.

7) Set a specific amount of time that you are willing to spend with a prospect before moving on to the next one. Know when to quit.

8) Determine not to sell your prospects on features or benefits. Sell them on the problem, and they will demand the solution.

9) Find a way to separate your prospecting from your selling, and determine to keep them separate.

10) Commit to treating your prospects to a non-confrontational buying experience by using the No Objection Selling process:
   1) Discover Their Want
   2) Reveal the Problems
   3) Reveal Their Conditions
   4) Reveal the Solution
   5) Settle the Details

Chapter Fifteen

♦

Versatility

No Objection Selling Methods Vary But The Principles Do Not

> If you give a man a fish, you've fed him for a day. But if you teach him how to fish, he'll patronize your bait shop.

Would you send your prospect over to your competitor if you knew that you did not have what your prospect wanted, and your competitor did?

This question brings to mind the scene from *Miracle on 34th Street*, where the Macy's Santa was doing just that. Many of the stuffed shirts at Macy's were beside themselves with shock and outrage, until they discovered that their sales took an immediate spike as word got out that Macy's was there to unselfishly serve their customers.

I realize that this is only a scene from a fictional movie, nevertheless, I have done this very thing myself, and I have no regrets.

If someone wants something, and I do not have it, then I honestly have no desire to sell something he or she does not want just for the sake of making a buck, even if I could easily do so.

The first time I heard Peter Daniels speak, he defined success as "The willingness to bear pain." In his Australian accent, with the "r" sound nearly silent, it sounded like he said "the willingness to be a pain," so he repeated by stating, "I didn't say *be* a pain, I said *bear* pain."

In grasping the No Objection Selling philosophy, the bottom line is to acquire an attitude that compels you to always seek to do what is best for your prospects. You may refer a sale to a competitor from time to time, or lose a few deals to salespeople who are more aggressive. Just the thought of this may be painful to you. Are you willing to let those sales go, along with the egocentric beliefs about selling, in order to achieve a higher level of professionalism and performance? Are you willing to bear this pain and stop *being* a pain to your prospects? Only you can answer these questions for yourself.

If I could send one message to all buyers, it would be that the harder someone tries to get you to make a hasty decision, the more reason that person has for not wanting you to reflect on what you are getting into.

If you agree with the above statement, then you have a No Objection Selling mindset, and although urgency is preferred by the salesperson, you must understand that some prospects want soaking time so they may feel comfortable with their buying decision. Respect and accommodate their wants, and your prospects will appreciate this and instinctively feel that they want to buy from you, because people desire to do business with professionals who understand their problems and are willing to serve them by helping them solve those problems.

Additionally, customers have learned that satisfaction is a much better feeling than regret, but either feeling will last as long as they own their purchase, and beyond.

Striving to understand your buyer's perspective is not sympathy, it is a servant attitude that lowers the normal resistance buyers take into a sales encounter, which is the resistance they put up to protect themselves from salespeople who want to make a sale more than they want to do what is best for their prospect.

♦ Prospects Can Resist or Assist ♦

Remember, prospects will resist you if you try to take them somewhere they do not want to go, but they will assist you if you try to take them where they do wish to go. Salespeople who exclusively use No Objection Selling can hold their heads high and be proud of the way they serve their prospects, their customers, and their employers. The public will reward them, much to the detriment of their less enlightened rivals.

I pointed out in Chapter One that this is not simply a book about selling; it is a tool for selling my ideas to you. I do not claim to have the manipulative powers with which so many sales gurus credit them selves, nor do I pretend to be able to turn someone's no into a yes, although I do know how to quickly and easily find more yeses.

The ten components of No Objection Selling make up a formula for developing a systematic, step-by-step, by-the-numbers approach for quickly and easily attracting predisposed buyers, sorting out the non-buyers, and helping those that are mentally prepared to buy to choose to buy from you when appropriate, which, if the formula is applied correctly, will be more often than not.

Depending on what is right for your prospects at the time, some may choose not to buy. If this is the case, use what I call patient persistence, and accept their decision not to buy, but keep the door open to selling them at a later date when their situation or their wants warrant it.

Always put in place a mechanism for getting additional business from your customers, because the best prospect is and always will be a satisfied customer.

In addition, develop a process for getting lots of good quality referrals, even from quality prospects who may have declined to buy from you, because, as Peter Daniels says, "Ornithological species of identical plumes tend to congregate in the closest proximity." (Birds of a feather flock together.)

I have found that there is a different way of structuring a No Objection Selling approach for nearly every product or service, and when all of the components of such a system are brought together and put into effect, you can get superior sales results from average and below average people where selling skills, experience and knowledge are concerned.

If you are a leader in a sales organization, one of the biggest benefits of needing only average people is that a very profitable sales force can be developed without ever having to depend on sales superstars. This works in your favor because prima donnas tend to take full advantage of any leverage they can get over their employers. More-over, there are a whole lot more average people out there available for hire than there are superstars.

On the other hand, if you are a sales person, the advantage to you is that you can experience a rather quick improvement in your sales success without having to invest months or years into memorizing rebuttals and perfecting closing techniques. No Objection Selling will either make you a better salesperson, or make your selling easier, or both.

♦ **Some Examples NOS Success** ♦

Although the No Objection Selling process was developed to sell property and casualty insurance, it has since been successfully applied to many different products and services in many industries.

For example, within two weeks of implementing NOS, a real estate agent was able to find buyers for homes that had been sitting on the market for up to a year. This happened during a flat period where there was no upturn in the market, except for his personal sales. In addition, the sellers were thrilled because not only were they able to finally sell their homes, they received exactly the amount they wanted. Price did not have to be compromised.

After implementing NOS among their telemarketers, a bank that provides auto loan refinancing was able to experience a tremendous increase in the number of loan applications, such that they had to tighten their underwriting to reduce the number of closings due to a staff size that was unprepared to handle the sudden influx of qualified applicants.

One company that sells two-for-one deals for upscale restaurants experienced an immediate five-fold increase in orders once NOS was implemented. The VP of sales was so astonished that he refused to believe the deals were legitimate until he personally began to follow up and verified that the new sales were indeed solid.

No Objection Selling works because it allows salespeople to quickly and easily reach more potential buyers on a favorable basis, which results in more and better selling opportunities.

◆ Selling Versus Advertising ◆

Do you remember Pets.com, the sock puppet guys? They spent millions and millions of investor dollars on advertising, but where are they now? More importantly, where is their investor's money now?

We all know the answer to that one. Their money is in the bank accounts of advertising executives. In fact, those same people revitalized the sock puppet for another project several years later. They're *still* laughing all the way to the bank.

This proves that creative advertising can be very lucrative...for advertising people. What most business owners do not realize is that the majority of advertising agencies are spending their client's money on creative and expensive ways to make their *advertising* famous. What they ought to be doing is finding practical and affordable ways for making their client's *brands* famous.

Sales are what make the cash register ring, and while advertising is a gamble on tomorrow, a sale is what you put in the bank today.

Please do not misunderstand, I am not against advertising, it is a necessary function of just about any company. To provide value, however, it must serve the correct purpose.

A marching band maneuvers expertly on a football field for the purpose of looking good. They get cheers and may even get an award...for looking good. A football team, on the other hand, maneuvers on the same field for the purpose of scoring touchdowns and winning games. Do you go to football games to root for the marching band or the football team? Which is the reason for the other?

The Pets.com ads looked good; they even got cheers and awards...for looking good. They just did not win in the marketplace.

Do you want your company to look good, or do you want it to win?

In war, it is not the spit and polished soldiers who perform with perfect timing and precision on the parade field that make the difference, it is the troops who fight and win the battles. Which do you want on *your* team?

♦ Quit Polishing the Brass and ♦ Bring Out the Big Guns!

Unlike advertising, which you have to buy over and over again to maintain the desired result, a powerful selling system can have lasting effects that will benefit your company's bottom line well after most of your expensive ads are long forgotten. What's more, developing and implementing an engineered selling system is usually much less expensive than even a modest advertising campaign.

So invest the time to apply the principles in this book to your sales approach, and I am certain that you will be enjoying the benefits of No Objection Selling for many years to come.

Epilogue

♦

The Final Step

> *"Life is not a dress rehearsal."*
> **Peter J. Daniels**

Throughout this book, I have stressed the importance of believing, deciding, and committing. The steps in this book require you to create new, good habits, and never allow an exception to occur. Most people lack the self discipline to force themselves to do this. Do not be one of them.

I promised that if you completed each step in this book, you would receive the benefits of No Objection Selling as described in Chapter One. Here is the final step:

Take the list of ten key components of No Objection Selling found at the end of Chapter Fourteen and make several copies to keep handy. Memorize them, refer to them often, and believe in them. Structure your sales approach around them and act accordingly.

Also, right here and now, mark your calendar to reread this book in thirty days. Do this every month for the next six months, at which time you can back it off to every ninety days.

Remember, a person is not wise for understanding, as there are many very educated people struggling to make a decent living. Neither are people wise for believing, for many people believe the words of great and successful business leaders but fail to implement and benefit from their teachings. Nor are people wise for agreeing, for the world is full of yes-men who accomplish nothing.

The true indicator of a wise person is whether or not he or she does what needs to be done.

To quote Peter Daniels, "When all is said and done, there's usually much more said than done."

Doing is what matters, and is what will give you the results you are looking for. So take the steps as instructed in this book, and you will reap the rewards you richly deserve.

About the Author

Paul David French discovered the principles of No Objection Selling as a result of an intensive self development program he undertook to overcome his extremely analytical approach and introverted style. He quickly become the top producer of the largest property and casualty insurance company in the State of Michigan during his rookie year in spite of his lack of sales experience, knowledge, skills or contacts. Paul's implementation of No Objection Selling also allowed him to achieve his company's highest client retention and lowest loss ratio simultaneously, giving him the most profitable book of business per premium dollar in the company.

Since then, Paul has consulted with many business owners and top executives across the U.S. and is the founder and president of NOS Marketing, a marketing and consulting firm that specializes in developing unique sales approaches and providing sales training based upon the principles of No Objection Selling.

You can contact Paul by sending an email to: pfrench@noobjectionselling.com

Or visit: www.noobjectionselling.com

Also by Paul David French:
$ix Figure Selling

As you read each of the fifty short chapters, you'll expose your mind to powerful success principles as well as the anecdotes and examples which demonstrate their practical application for achieving spectacular success in selling.

One of the most important success principles is humor; the ability to enjoy life, to laugh, and to make others laugh. Combining humor and useful information together results in a more immediate, stronger, and longer lasting effect.

- Learn the powerful psychological technique that will give anyone the irresistible power of overwhelming self confidence.

- Discover the biggest mistake salespeople make in selling and how to avoid it forever.

- Read about powerful negotiation weapons of the world's top negotiators.

- Uncover the secret to Jerry Seinfeld's marketing genius.

- Receive success advice from the most important man of the twentieth century.

- Discover how to achieve an unfair competitive advantage.

- And much, much more ...

"I personally used the techniques in this book to become the top producer of a multi-billion dollar sales organization during my rookie year. Now it's your turn to use these powerful ideas to break into the world of Six Figure Selling!"

Order at www.noobjectionselling.com